Divination
of
God

The Obscure Ancient Tool
of Prophecy Revealed

Divination
of
God

The Obscure Ancient Tool
of Prophecy Revealed

Shelley Kaehr, Ph.D.

We Publish Books
United States of America

We Publish Books
P.O. Box 1814
Rancho Mirage, CA 92270

www.WePublishBooks.com
E-mail: WePublishBooks@gmail.com

Library of Congress Cataloging in Publication Data:
Library of Congress Control Number: 2005932571

Kaehr, Shelley
Divination Of God: The Obscure Ancient Tool of Prophecy Revealed

Printed in the United States and London

Cover designed by Rhonda Clifton Lyons
Cover Photograph by Captain E. Larry VanHoose

Divination Of God: The Obscure Ancient Tool of Prophecy Revealed /
by Shelley Kaehr, Ph.D.

    1. **BODY, MIND & SPIRIT** / Divination / General OCC005000
    2. **RELIGION** / Bible / Prophecies REL006140
    3. **RELIGION** / Mysticism REL047000

Bibliography and Indexed

ISBN-13: 978-1-929841-20-2 Hardcover
ISBN-10: 1-929841-20-5   Hardcover

ISBN-13: 978-1-929841-19-6 Paperback
ISBN-10: 1-929841-19-1   Paperback

First Printing, 2005

We Publish Books

ʊable Of Contents

Acknowledgements

As always, this project would never have come to fruition without the support of many people.

First, to Jennifer Theis who gave me my first copy of the beautiful book *The Alchemist*, and Rhonda Clifton Lyons for believing in the project from the beginning.

To Linnea and David Armstrong, George Skurla, Jr., Helen McCrea, Father Paul Keenan, Mary Greer, Charlie Comstock, Shannon Randall, Mark Thurston, Laura McGillivray, Grant Lean, Hugo Janco Caceres, Neal, Cheli and Lauren Broussard, I am in awe of your knowledge and thankful for your willingness to share it with me.

Finally to my family, Mickey, Gail and Mark whose love and support allow me to write, I am deeply grateful.

To Joe Crosson
In Loving Memory

Introduction

(...) I shall speak out freely, and I shall express my various sayings among you (...) (.. those who would understand parables and riddles, and those who would penetrate the origins of knowledge, along with those who hold fast to the wonderful mysteries ...) *Dead Sea Scrolls, The Book of Secrets*, 1Q27, 4Q299-301,4Q301 F1

I received a copy of the beautiful book *The Alchemist* shortly after my book *Edgar Cayce's Guide to Gemstones, Minerals, Metals & More* was released. I was glued to every word, especially as I read about a divination tool consisting of two stones with Biblical origins called the Urim and Thummim. I instantly felt I was to explore the topic further.

A few days later, a wonderful friend and client sent me an e-mail telling me she was ordering the Cayce book, and serendipitously attached several pages on Urim and Thummim and the impact they had on the development of Mormonism, which is something we will explore later in the book. These were the same Urim and Thummim I had just read about the week before. The coincidences were mounting quickly and I began to do more research. Little by little, as in so many of my projects, I felt I was being led to write this.

Initially, I thought the book should be all about the Urim and Thummim of the Bible, yet after doing hours of research, I determined the book should also focus on other complimentary oracles from civilizations throughout the world. Some of this information gives a fascinating look into the minds of humankind throughout the ages.

My goal for the book is to allow you to accompany me on my own inner journey of discovery to trace the origins and spiritual importance of the Urim and Thummim and its possible links to earlier times.

In the last part of the book, I'll show you the materials you can use to create your own oracle, revitalizing this ancient Biblical tool, and teach you how to apply it to bring greater clarity and wisdom to your life.

I hope this writing will somehow play a small part in unveiling a previously obscured mystery to benefit all who are able and willing to use it.

In Peace,

Shelley Kaehr, Ph.D.
July 21, 2005

Part 1

BIBLICAL DIVINATION

"And thou shalt put in the breastplate of judgment the Urim and Thummim..."

Exodus: 28:30

One

LIGHTS AND PERFECTIONS

n the following pages, you'll be reading about an ancient divination tool hidden in the Bible that will enable you to have a more conscious experience of the divine connection we all have to our Creator, and one that I find absolutely fascinating.

Over the centuries, the Christian Church has traditionally banned divination instruments of all kinds, labeling them as evil. *("For rebellion is like the sin of divination, and arrogance like the evil of idolatry..." I Samuel 15:23)* Yet, there is one such instrument that exists in all versions of the Bible that stands out as one of the only direct ways for man to communicate with God, called the Urim and Thummim. The fact that it exists at all and has been there all along is exciting to me.

There is an old saying that God gives us everything we need. The problem is we may or may not notice it, or be ready for it. By looking at this ancient tool in new light, we allow our Creator the opportunity to communicate with us with greater clarity than ever before.

In Hebrew, Urim means "Lights" and Thummim means "Perfections," which could relate to the illumination or "light" you receive when you have a clear link to your Creator and "perfection" as the correct and profound wisdom of God.

I first learned about Urim and Thummim after my book *Edgar Cayce's Guide to Gemstones, Minerals, Metals and More* had already been published. In that work, I described the stones in the breastplate of the high priest, and unfortunately, was not aware of the special stones that lay just behind the others that the High Priests of Israel used to speak to God.

As I mentioned briefly in the introduction, a friend gave me a copy of the beautifully written book *The Alchemist*, which is a Biblical metaphor about a shepherd boy who travels to Egypt in search of hidden treasure. In the book, he exchanges some of his sheep for two stones called Urim and Thummim used to offer him wisdom and direction in times of need.

When I read the passage, a feeling of great knowingness rushed over me and I knew I was going to write a book and show this to people so it would be a more readily accessible tool for a divine connection to God.

The Breastplate

Before we get into the Urim and Thummim, we should discuss the breastplate and its uses. In Exodus, the Lord commanded Moses to deliver the Israelites from Egypt and gave him the Ten Commandments and other Laws on Mount Sinai, including the exact specifications of how the church, or Tabernacle, was to be constructed, and how it should be decorated. There were also specific instructions about the garments the priests would wear which included a breastplate to be worn initially by Moses' brother Aaron, and all subsequent High Priests of Israel.

In the photo toward the end of the book, you'll see roughly what some would say the mysterious breastplate would have looked like. It had twelve stones embedded in it, each representing one of the twelve tribes of Israel.

As I discussed in the Cayce book, scholars have continually debated on the exact identity of the each of the stones that were used. The truth is that nobody will ever really know for sure what they were. For this writing, I am using the exact stones mentioned in the King James version of the Bible, and will continue to refer to the King James for the remainder of the book:

> "And you shall put settings of stones in it, four rows of
> stones: The first row shall be a sardius, a topaz, and a
> carbuncle; this shall be the first row, the second row
> shall be an emerald, a sapphire, and a diamond, the
> third row, a ligure, an agate, and an amethyst, and the
> forth row, a beryl, an onyx and a jasper. They shall be
> set in gold settings. And the stones shall have the names
> of the sons of Israel, twelve according to their names,
> like the engravings of a signet, each one with its own
> name; they shall be according to the twelve tribes."
> Exodus 28:17-21

In addition to the twelve stones representing the tribes, the priest
would also wear engraved onyx stones on his shoulders with each of
the tribes names written on them – six tribes per stone:

> "And thou shalt take two onyx stones, and grave on
> them the names of the children of Israel: Six of their
> names on one stone, and the other six names of the rest
> on the other stone, according to their birth. With the
> work of an engraver in stone, like the engravings of a
> signet, shalt thou engrave the two stones with the names
> of the children of Israel: Thou shalt make them to be set
> in ouches of gold. And thou shalt put the two stones
> upon the shoulders of the ephod for stones of memorial
> unto the children of Israel: and Aaron shall bear their
> names before the Lord upon his two shoulders for a
> memorial." Exodus 28:9-12

Nobody knows for sure what these stones did, although some believe
the onyx stones were an oracle themselves and would illuminate from
time to time. When the right onyx lit up, it indicated God's answer
was positive, or 'yes', and when the left was illuminated it indicated a
'no' response.

The exact identity of the twelve tribes is also revealed in Exodus:

> "Now these are the names of the children of Israel, which came into Egypt; every man and his household came with Jacob. Reuben, Simeon, Levi, and Judah. Issachar, Zebulun, and Benjamin, Dan, and Naphtali, Gad and Asher. And all the souls that came out of the loins of Jacob were seventy souls: for Joseph was in Egypt already."   Exodus 1: 1-5

The stones in the breastplate were in and of themselves an oracle, according to one scholar I interviewed. In his interpretation, the stones were carved with letters from the Hebrew alphabet and would occasionally light up and someone would transcribe God's messages to the priest. What those letters were, though is also unknown.

Another version of that story is that the twelve stones would light up prior to combat to indicate the Lord's favor and the successful outcome of the battle, but eventually God became displeased as the Children of Israel fell out of favor, so the twelve stones stopped becoming illuminated.

URIM & THUMMIM

"And thou shalt put in the breastplate of judgment the Urim and Thummim; and they will be upon Aaron's heart when he goeth in before the Lord: and Aaron shall bear the judgment of the children of Israel upon his heart before the Lord continually."
Exodus: 28:30

hen God spoke to Moses on Mount Sinai, He gave him detailed instructions on the duties of the Priests, and the breastplate, yet only briefly mentioned the Urim and Thummim.

Some scholars conclude there was a pouch of some kind sitting behind the breastplate where the Urim and Thummim were safely tucked away. The challenge is that the concept is only mentioned a few other times in the Bible, and each reference is extremely vague, just like it is with the breastplate.

After the Tabernacle is built, Moses consecrates his brother Aaron into the priesthood and places the breastplate, Urim and Thummim, and other priestly garments on him:

> "And Moses brought Aaron and his sons, and washed them with water. And he put upon him the coat, and girded him with the girdle, and clothed him with the robe, and put the ephod upon him, and he girded him with the curious girdle of the ephod, and bound it unto

him therewith. And he put the breastplate upon him: also he put in the breastplate the Urim and the Thummim. And he put the mitre upon his head, also upon the mitre, even upon his forefront, did he put the golden plate, the holy crown; as the LORD commanded Moses..." Leviticus 8:6-9

Urim was mentioned again when the Lord warned Moses of his pending death and he was asked to elevate Joshua's status among the Israelites:

"And he shall stand before Eleazar the priest, who shall ask counsel for him after the judgment of Urim before the Lord: at his word shall they go out, and at his word they shall come in, both he, and all the children of Israel with him, even all the congregation. And Moses did as the Lord commanded him: and he took Joshua, and set him before Eleazar the priest, and before all the congregation: And he laid his hands upon him, and gave him a charge, as the Lord commanded by the hand of Moses." Numbers 27:21-23

Eleazar, the priest, is asked to use the Urim to communicate with God and the blessing of Joshua cannot take place until this is done. Because it was initially a tool used only by the priest, the Urim and Thummim was later passed on to Levi in Deuteronomy as he was consecrated in the priesthood, and implies he proved himself and is therefore worthy:

"And of Levi he said, Let thy Thummim and thy Urim be with thy holy one, whom thou didst prove at Massah, and with whom thou didst strive at the waters of Meribah..." Deuteronomy 33:8

One passage that most profoundly reveals the use of Urim and Thummim comes when Saul attempts to communicate with the Lord:

> "And when Saul enquired of the LORD, the LORD
> answered him not, neither by dreams, nor by Urim, nor
> by prophets." I Samuel 28:6

This passage will be explored at length later in the book, yet out of context, it suggests that only the chosen could communicate with God using Urim and Thummim. This book will expand what was previously acceptable use of the tool to make it accessible for everyone, not just the chosen few.

In the books of Ezra and Nehemiah the Israelites return to Jerusalem after their Babylonian captivity. The governor, or 'Tirshatha,' requests a priest and Urim and Thummim to be used to determine who is a true Israelite and who is not, and until that is decided, does not want them to eat:

> "And the Tirshatha said unto them, that they should not
> eat of the most holy things, till there stood up a priest
> with Urim and with Thummim," Ezra 2:63

Again it is implied that the Urim and Thummim will provide the exact will of God in any situation and must be consulted before action can be taken. The same passage is repeated in Nehemiah, which some say is an exact replica of the book of Ezra:

> "And the Tirshatha said unto them, that they should not
> eat of the most holy things, till there stood up a priest
> with Urim and Thummim," Nehemiah 7:65

In the Hebrew Bible, Ezra and Nehemiah are included in just one book. It is interesting to note that although the governor requests a priest, there is never another reference to it again, which makes me think that something is missing – perhaps an entire section – to explain how this issue was settled.

One of the most telling passages comes from the Septuagint, which is Greek version of the Hebrew Scriptures dating back to the 3rd century in the following:

> "Then Saul prayed to the Lord, the God of Israel, "Give
> me the right answer." "Why have you not answered
> your servant today? If the fault is in me or my son
> Jonathan, respond with Urim, but if the men of Israel
> are not at fault, respond with Thummim." And
> Jonathan and Saul were taken by lot, and the men were
> cleared." I Samuel 14:41

The passage above suggests that the Urim and Thummim are clearly
used to make yes/no decisions and show that Saul considers it to be a
communication from the Lord. It also speaks of the drawing of lots,
another common practice we'll look at in the next chapter.

The King James Version of this is a bit different, calling the Urim and
Thummim a 'perfect lot':

> "Be ye on one side, and I and Jonathan my son will be
> on the other side, And the people said unto Saul, So
> what seemeth good unto thee. Therefore Saul said unto
> the Lord God of Israel, Give a perfect lot. And Saul
> and Jonathan were taken: but the people escaped."
> I Samuel 14:41

One other theory I heard is in reference to a modern use for Urim and
Thummim within the Catholic faith. I'm sure you remember the recent
passing of Pope John Paul II. During this time the church goes
through a strict ritual for selection of the new Pontiff which includes
sequestering the Cardinals while discussion, debate and several rounds
of voting take place.

After each vote, the ballots are burned in the fire, which sends smoke
signals out into the world. If the smoke is white, it means a new Pope
has been chosen, if it is black, colored by a chemical they add to it,
then the decision has not yet been made.

One of my devout Catholic friends mentioned this when I told him of the Urim and Thummim and said that it was his understanding that this ritual was a modern form of this because it is through God's word, received by the Cardinals in deep contemplation and prayer, that the Pope is selected. Interesting theory, especially timely too, since the process is still so fresh in our minds.

I asked my Catholic Priest friend about this and he disagreed with it and said the smoke is not considered communication with God, but merely a form of human communication. He did acknowledge that the selection of Pope is certainly inspired by God.

My initial image of the Urim and Thummim as two stones, one black, one white, probably came from the beautiful imagery of *The Alchemist*, however as my research progressed, as you will see later in the book, I have come to a new broader understanding of this tool.

The lack of definite information about Urim and Thummim and the way it appears in passages as if the reader should know what is meant by it, makes me wonder if there was once more information about Urim and Thummim that was lost on the cutting room floor in the Council of Nicea in 325 A.D. and during other subsequent Biblical edits through the ages.

Some of the first documented revisions to the Bible were made in 325 A.D. when a group of scholars began a debate over the origins of Christ and changed some of the original writings to reflect the fact that Christ and God were one and the same.

After the discovery of the Dead Sea Scrolls between 1947 and 1956, more information has surfaced suggesting that key documents in the original Scriptures may have been altered or deleted completely in order to satisfy the needs of the Church at any given time.

It seems strange to me that the Lord would mention something, yet not describe in detail what it is and exactly how it was used. Of course, the Bible is filled with allegorical and symbolic information not readily understood by the novice, yet despite that fact, you would think there would be some type of description beyond what is currently offered.

Could it be that at one time a detailed description existed about this very powerful and ancient tool? I believe that is highly probable. Whether we'll find it or not, remains to be seen.

Biblical Divination References

In the next section, we will take a brief look at several other types of Biblical divination in the Bible and compare them with the Urim and Thummim. As you will see, many of them are reserved for the few and most are not direct forms of communication with the divine.

Three

DRAWING OF LOTS

"The lot causeth contentions to cease, and parteth between the mighty."   **Proverbs 18:18**

here are several places in the Bible where certain kinds of divination are considered acceptable, including the drawing of lots, mentioned briefly in the last chapter, which was a relatively common occurrence in the Bible. Drawing lots is a process where any material object is used to make random selections that determine the outcome, or fate, of something.

The process of using the Urim and Thummim is nothing more than a divine casting of lots with only two choices offered – a yes, or a no.

The term comes from the abbreviated version of the word lottery, which most of us are probably quite familiar with, although in ancient times, lottery did not necessarily mean you'd win millions, but it could mean the difference between life and death.

Aaron drew lots to determine which of two goats would be used as scapegoat:

> "And Aaron shall cast lots upon the two goats; one lot for the Lord, and the other lot for the scapegoat. And Aaron shall bring the goat upon which the Lord's lot fell and offer him for a sin offering. But the goat, on which the lot fell to be the scapegoat, shall be presented alive

before the Lord to make an atonement with him, and to
let him go for a scapegoat into the wilderness."
Leviticus 16: 8-10

One of the most dramatic events using the casting of lots occurs in the
New Testament as a replacement for Judas is chosen to be apostle:

"And they prayed, and said, Thou, Lord, which knowest
the hearts of all men, shew whether of these two thou
has chosen, That he may take part of this ministry and
apostleship, from which Judas by transgression fell, that
he might go to his own place. And they gave forth their
lots; and the lot fell upon Matthias; and he was
numbered with the eleven apostles." Acts 1: 24-26

Casting of lots determines the fate or destiny of something, and clearly
there are places in the Bible where the Lord requested these processes
be followed to determine the desired outcome. One important casting
of lots determined the inheritance of the land to the tribes of Israel:

"And ye shall divide the land by lot for an inheritance
among your families: and to the more ye shall give the
more inheritance, and to the fewer ye shall give the less
inheritance: every man's inheritance shall be in the
place where his lot falleth: according to the tribes of
your fathers ye shall inherit." Numbers 33:54

One of the shortest but most significant books of the Bible is the book
of Esther, the story of the heroic Jewish woman who became a queen
and stood up to the King to spare the Jewish race from elimination by
the hand of an enemy. The book of Esther is devoted to the story of
lots, called Pur:

"Because Haman the son of Jammedatha, the Agagite,
the enemy of all the Jews, had devised against the Jews
to destroy them, and had cast Pur, that is, the lot, to
comsume them, and to destroy them," Esther 9:24

In that case, the casting of the lots was used, not as divine connection, but as man's justification to do whatever he wants to do. Haman had plans to destroy the people until Esther intervened on their behalf. To this day the events called The Days of Purim are celebrated annually on the 14th day of the Hebrew month of Adar, which is February-March, to commemorate the deliverance of the Jewish people:

> "Wherefore they called these days Purim after the name of Pur." Esther 9:26

> "And that these days should be remembered and kept throughout every generation, every family, every province, and every city; and that these days of Purim should not fail from among the Jews, nor the memorial of them perish from their seed." Esther 9:28

It seems fitting to call the festival 'Purim' since it was through fate or lots that the people were spared. The Book of Esther also had influence on other cultures as well, including the Assyrians, Babylonians and Persians.

The Assyrian New Year celebration was called Puru, and in Babylonia it was called Puhru. One scholar noted the story of Esther replayed in ancient Babylonian texts with Mordecai as Marduk, and Esther as Ishtar. Much about Marduk is written in the Zecharia Sitchen books.

Because the King was Persian decent, it's not surprising the Persian Purdighan is the word representing the New Year's Feast.

The process of casting lots is obviously Biblically accepted because it is still used today in the Catholic Church during the process of selecting a Pope. Lots are drawn and Cardinals are randomly selected to count and collect the ballots during the conclave.

Even the Dalai Lama used a lottery to determine his successor, for the same divine reasons.

The lottery system is also used in modern times to determine everything from military drafts to court case outcomes.

One of the more interesting stories I heard was about John Wesley, founder of the Methodist Church who used a lot system to decide whether or not to get married. He took out three pieces of paper and wrote marry, not this year and don't ever consider it again on them and then drew, asking for God's guidance. Apparently, he was instructed by the lot not to marry, and because it was God's will, he never did.

If the Urim and Thummim are but a special form of lots, it is easy to see why this form of divination is authorized by the Bible and can be expanded and applied to our own daily use.

And as far as the ancient lots systems are concerned, the next time you buy a quick pick, think about the long and complex history that brought you to that convenience store and feel thankful you'll only be out a dollar or two if things don't work out. It could be a lot worse!

ℱour

DREAMS

"For a dream cometh through the multitude of business; and a fool's voice is known by multitude of words." Ecclesiastes 5:3

n a more indirect form of communication, God occasionally spoke to people in dreams as in Genesis, when he speaks to King Abimelech and reprimands him for taking Abraham's wife, Sarah:

> "But God came to Abimelech in a dream by night, and said to him, Behold, thou art but a dead man, for the woman which thou hast taken; for she is a man's wife," Genesis 20:3

The King fortunately redeems himself and is forgiven:

> "And God said to him in a dream, Yea, I know that thou didst this in the integrity of thy heart..." Genesis 20:6

One of the most interesting stories of the dreamers of the Bible is the story of Joseph in the Book of Genesis. Joseph was his father's favorite son, which made his eleven brothers very jealous. One night, he dreamed he was in the corn fields and his sheaf rose above the others and his brothers bowed before him. He told the dream to the family and the brothers became extremely angry:

"What is this dream that thou hast dreamed? Shall I and thy mother and thy brethren indeed come to bow down ourselves to thee to the earth?" Genesis 37:10

The jealous brothers sold Joseph into slavery and he was sent to Egypt where he was eventually falsely accused of adultery and imprisoned. While in jail, Joseph interpreted dreams for two prisoners. One of the prisoners was Pharaoh's former butler who had a dream about three branches with grapes and making wine to serve the Pharaoh:

"And Joseph said unto him, This is the interpretation of it: The three branches are three days: Yet within three days shall Pharaoh life up think head, and restore thee unto thy place: and thou shalt deliver Pharaoh's cup into his hand, *after the former manner when thous wast his butler." Genesis 40:12*

The other prisoner had a dream that he was carrying a basket full of meat for the Pharaoh and it was eaten by a bunch of birds. Joseph predicted his fate was sealed and that he would be executed in three days:

"And he restored the chief butler unto his butlership again; and he gave the cup into Pharaoh's hand: But he hanged the chief baker: as Joseph had interpreted to them. Yet did not the chief butler remember Joseph, but forgat him." Genesis 40:21-22

Eventually, Joseph was called to interpret dreams for Pharaoh and because of his accuracy, was totally restored to grace:

"And Pharaoh said unto Joseph, I have dreamed a dream, and there I non that can interpret it: and I have heard say of thee, that thou canst understand a dream to interpret it. And Joseph answered Pharaoh, saying, It is not in my: God shall give Pharoah and answer of peace." Genesis 41:15-16

Other Biblical prophets also possessed the gift of dream interpretation including Daniel, who was approached similarly by King Jehoiakim of Judah to interpret his dream:

> "Daniel answered in the presence of the king, and said, The secret which the king hath demanded cannot the wise men, the astrologers, the magicians, the soothsayers, shew unto the king; But there is a God in heaven that revealeth secrets, and maketh known to the king Nebuchadnezzar what shall be in the latter days. Thy dream and the visions of thy head upon thy bed are these." Daniel 2: 27-28

God communicated through dreams in the New Testament as well:

> "But while he thought on these things, behold, the angel of the Lord appeared unto him in a dream, saying, Joseph, thou son of David, fear not to take unto thee Mary thy wife: for that which is conceived in her is of the Holy Ghost." Matthew 1:20

> "And being warned of God in a dream that they should not return to Herod, they departed into their own country another way. And when they were departed, behold, the angel of the Lord appeareth to Joseph in a dream, saying, Arise, and take the young child and his mother and flee into Egypt..." Matthew 2:12-13

> "But when Herod was dead, behold, an angel of the Lord appeareth in a dream to Joseph in Egypt." Matthew 2:19

> "...being warned of God in a dream, he turned aside into the parts of Galillee: and he came and dwelt in a city called Nazareth." Matthew 2:22-23

Whether God was offering warnings or prophecies, dreams appear to be an acceptable form of communication with the divine. It differs from the Urim and Thummim though, because it is only through symbols and is not a direct line to the Creator.

Five

THE ARK OF THE COVENANT

"And Moses wrote this law, and delivered it unto the priests the sons of Levi, which bare the ark of the covenant of the Lord, and unto all the elders of Israel."

Deuteronomy 31:9

Clearly the Biblical legend of the Arc of the Covenant must be cited in any writing about Biblical prophecy and divination.

The Tabernacle was constructed through clear instructions Moses received from the Lord. It consisted of two or three rooms (there is another scholarly debate over this issue), one being the Holy of Holies, which could only be entered into once a year by the High Priest.

The priest would carry a string with goat's blood on it into the Holy of Holies, and if it turned white when he came out, it meant that the sins of the children of Israel had been forgiven, if it remained red, the Lord was displeased.

When the priest entered the Holy of Holies, he was expected to be completely pure in thought and deed. If he had even one impure thought, he would be struck dead instantly by the Divine flame. As a chain was attached to the priest's ankle before he entered the Holy of Holies in case he had to be dragged out post mortem as a precaution.

There is evidence to suggest that the Urim and Thummim were with the priest when he approached the tabernacle for his annual visit. In one passage, Aaron was instructed to wear the Urim and Thummim when he went before the Lord:

> "...the Urim and Thummim...shall be upon Aaron's
> heart when he goeth before the Lord: and Aaron shall
> bear the judgment of the children of Israel upon his
> heart before the Lord continually." Exodus 28:30

To me, this passage implies that the Urim and Thummim are more than simple instruments for answering yes or no, and may actually function as an extension of the Ark itself. When the priest is not in the Holy of Holies, he can still hear God's word by having them near his heart, as if Urim and Thummim were like an extension of the annual visit to the Tabernacle. Once a year, the priest would go before The Almighty, yet continually the Urim and Thummim would rest on his heart as a spiritual thermometer to gauge the righteous temperature of the children of Israel.

The arc itself was said to be two and a half cubits long, by one and a half cubits wide and one cubit tall. Inside this sacred vessel was the second copy of the Ten Commandments (because Moses broke the first set – *Exodus 32:19*) and manna from the Lord. It was overlaid with gold and on the top; two cherubs sat facing each other between the mercy seat where God would appear:

> "And there I will meet with thee, and I will commune
> wit thee from above the mercy seat, from between the
> two cherubim which are upon the ark of the testimony,
> of all things which I will give thee in commandment
> unto the children of Israel," Exodus 25:21

There is a veil of mystery surrounding the whereabouts of the Ark today. Some scholars believe it was destroyed by the Babylonians, while others say it was removed to Ethiopia hundreds of years ago. The legend says that Queen Sheba of Ethiopia traveled to Jerusalem and gave birth to King Solomon's son, Mehelik. The Queen returned to Africa, raised their son, and when he was grown, he traveled to meet his father who offered to make him King. Mehelik wanted to return to his home, however, so Solomon built a replica of the Ark and asked some of his men to accompany Mehelik on his journey. According to the tale, the replica was left behind and the real Ark remains in Ethiopia today, hidden within the grounds of the Church of Mary Zion in a town called Axum.

The area is supposedly heavily guarded by a holy man who undertakes the charge for his entire life. Witnesses have seen a building with a metal fence around it that exists there today, yet nobody knows for sure what is in there. When the guard is asked if he can leave, he supposedly says he cannot, so whatever he's guarding must be important!

If someone was to actually open the box, nobody knows what would happen to them. As seen in *Raiders of the Lost Ark*, the force could unleash a power previously unknown to man, although Hollywood does have a way of dramatizing any event!

The book of Revelation offers a glimpse into that possibility:

> "And the temple of God was opened in heaven, and there was seen in his temple the ark of his testament: and there were lightnings, and voices, and thunderings, and an earthquake, and great hail." Revelation 11:19

Regardless of where it is today, the Ark does represent a direct communication with God and for that reason is an important part of this study, however, we cannot access the Ark and it was not direct communication. The priest was the only person privy to it, and even then we are not certain of how the Lord appeared. Was the Ark an instrument which the Lord channeled energy through, or did He actually appear on the mercy seat? Either way, it differs from Urim and Thummim, although it may be an extension of that connection.

"Hear my cry, O God; attend unto my prayer."

Psalm 61:1

Six

DIRECT COMMUNICATION WITH THE CREATOR

Throughout the ages people have had a yearning to communicate with the Creator. The Bible is certainly no exception, and in many instances, God answered, or even appeared without warning to speak to the faithful. The first evidence of this appears in the book of Genesis:

> "And the Lord God commanded the man, saying, Of every tree of the garden thou mayest freely eat: But of the tree of the knowledge of good and evil, thou shalt not eat of it: For in the day that thou eatest therof thou shalt surely die." Genesis 2:16-17

The Lord also spoke directly to Moses:

> "And when the Lord saw that he turned aside to see, God called unto him out of the midst of the bush, and said, Moses, Moses. And he said, here am I." Exodus 3:4

> "And the Lord spake unto Moses in the wilderness of Sinai, in the tabernacle of the congregation, on the first day of the second month, in the second year after they were come out of the land of Egypt." Numbers 1:1

In one passage, Moses recognizes himself as a liaison between the people and God:

"The Lord talked with you face to face in the mount out of the midst of the fire, (I stood between the Lord and you at that time, to shew you the word of the Lord...) Deuteronomy 5:4-5

God often spoke directly to people at the door of the Tabernacle, and promised Moses he would meet him there:

"This shall be a continual burnt offering throughout your generations at the door of the tabernacle of the congregation before the Lord: where I will meet you, to speak there unto thee. And there I will meet with the children of Israel, and the tabernacle shall be sanctified by my glory." Exodus 29:42-43

In Numbers, Moses' brother Aaron and his sister, Miriam, become jealous because of his strong connection with the Lord:

"And Miriam and Aaron spake against Moses because of the Ethiopian woman whom he had married: for he had married...and they said, hath the Lord indeed spoken only by Moses? Hath he not spoken also by us? And the Lord heard it." Numbers 12:1-2

God was angered by their disrespect of Moses and appeared to tell them so:

"And the Lord came down in the pillar of the cloud, and stood in the door of the tabernacle, and called Aaron and Miriam: and they both came forth. And he said, Hear now my words: If there be a prophet among you, I the Lord will make myself known unto him in a vision and will speak unto him in a dream. My servant Moses is not so, who is faithful in all mine house. With him will I speak mouth to mouth, even apparently, and not in dark speeches; and the similitude of the Lord shall he behold: wherefore then were ye not afraid to speak

against my servant Moses? And the anger of the Lord
was kindled against them; and he departed. And the
cloud departed from off the tabernacle."
Numbers 12:5-10

This passage is an interesting one because the Lord speaks not only
directly to Aaron and Miriam, but mentions his communications
through visions as well as in dreams.

In a later scene, the Lord materializes before Moses in a cloud inside
the Tabernacle:

"And the Lord appeared in the tabernacle in a pillar of a
cloud; and the pillar of the cloud stood over the door of
the tabernacle," Deuteronomy 31:15

Another amazing encounter with the Lord occurs when Isaiah has a
vision of him:

"I saw also the Lord sitting upon a throne, high and lifted up and his
train filled the temple." Isaiah 6:6

After he is cleansed and forgiven of his sins, God speaks to Isaiah and
commissions him to be a prophet:

"Also I heard the voice of the Lord, saying, Whom shall
I send, and who will go for us? Then said I, Here am I;
send me. And he said, Go and tell this people, Hear ye
indeed, but understand not; and see ye indeed, but
perceive not." Isaiah 6:8-9

Later God personally asks Jeremiah to write a book:

"The word that came to Jeremiah from the Lord saying,
Thus speaketh the Lord God of Israel, saying, Write
thee all the words that I have spoken unto thee in a
book." Jeremiah 30:1-2

Throughout the Old and New Testaments, communication with the higher power abounds so it should not be surprising that we are still reaching for that connection today. It is a timeless and universal desire, which will more than likely last for all eternity. But how can't he common man communicate with the Creator? In the previous passages, those who God chose to speak to were prophets and priests. Could the Urim and Thummim, the divine lots, be the answer? I think so.

Seven

ANGELIC COMMUNICATION

"For he shall give his angels charge over thee, to keep thee in all thy ways."   Psalms 91:11

or the past several years you've been hearing a lot about communicating with your angels and how angelic guides are helping each of us with all sorts of daily activities. Amazingly, as much criticism as certain New Age concepts seem to carry, angel communication is rarely condemned at all by the church.

Maybe that's because the term angel is used 283 times in the King James Version of the Bible – obviously too many examples to mention here. As you look through the various passages about angels in the Bible, they occur in such a positive light, it's no wonder that the thought of angels are acceptable to most people. In fact, you see surveys in the news media from time to time that reflect this to be true – people believe in angels!

This section will offer a very brief look at some of the Biblical angels who assisted their earthly counterparts.

Particularly throughout the entire book of Genesis, angels frequently communicated with people. One angel came to aid the distressed Hagar, Ishmael's mother, after she was banished from her house by Sarah:

"And the angel of the Lord said unto her, Return to thy

mistress, and submit thyself under her hands." Genesis
16:9

In the famous story of God's destruction of the sinful cities of Sodom
and Gomorrah, angels visited Lot, the only pure soul in the entire town
of Sodom, and assisted his escape before the entire city was destroyed:

> "And there came two angels to Sodom at even; and Lot
> sat in the gate of Sodom: and Lot seeing them rose up to
> meet them; and he bowed himself with his face toward
> the ground." Genesis 19:1

Before the Lord revealed himself to Moses, he sent an angel first in the
amazing account of the burning bush, and when Moses acknowledged
the angel's presence in spite of the fire, God rewarded him:

> "And the angel of the Lord appeared unto him in a
> flame of fire out of the midst of a bush: and he looked,
> and, behold, the bush burned with fire, and the bush
> was not consumed." Exodus3: 2

In Exodus, God promised to be the enemy of those who were enemies
of the people of Israel and proved it when he sent an angel to block the
passage of Balaam by standing in front of his donkey:

> "And God's anger was kindled because he went: and the
> angel of the Lord stood in the way for an adversary
> against him…And the ass saw the angel of the Lord
> standing in the way, and his sword drawn in his hand:
> and the ass turned aside out of the way, and went into
> the field…" Numbers 22:22-23

The passage is significant because Balaam was so arrogant, he failed to
see what his donkey saw – the angel of the Lord who had come to stop
him from going against God's will. So in essence, Biblical angels save
us from ourselves. We see that again in the book of Judges as angels
come to chastise the Israelites for their negligence:

"And an angel of the Lord came up from Gigal to
Bochim, and said, I made you to go up out of Egypt,
and have brought you unto the land which I sware unto
your fathers; and I said, I will never break my covenant
with you…but ye have not obeyed my voice: why have
ye done this?" Judges 2:1-2

Several other people in the Bible received angelic communication,
including Elijah, just as he was about to give up on life:

"And as he lay and slept under a juniper tree, behold,
then an angel touched him, and said unto him, Arise and
eat…And the angel of the Lord came again the second
time, and touched him, and said, Arise and eat; because
the journey is too great for thee." I Kings 19:5-7

And in I chronicles, King David is punished for counting the Israelites
and God sends his angels to inflict a plague over the land and is
eventually forgiven, so once again, we see the angel as an administer
of justice:

"And David lifted up his eyes, and saw the angel of the
Lord stand between the earth and the heaven…" I
Chronicles 21:16

And finally, Daniel is rescued from the lion's den because of his faith
in God:

" My God hath sent his angel, and hath shut the lions'
mouths, that they have not hurt me…" Daniel 6:22

The cherubs on the Ark of the Covenant have symbolic meaning as
God's messengers:

"One cherub on the end of this side, and another cherub
on the other end on that side: out of the mercy seat…"
Exodus 37:8

The two cherubs could represent some type of binary divinatory tool, yet it is not ever explicitly discussed, and we never see a place where they become animated and intervene with the messages delivered through the Ark. In the next section of the book, we will see similar representational systems used in other cultures that are reminiscent of these cherubs.

Angels have been an important part of our evolution for thousands of years. Whether saving us from impending doom or guiding us to live better lives, the connection we have to these divine beings continues and allows us to feel a closer connection to our Creator, yet it is indirect. The angel appears as the mediator between God and man, intervening on his behalf and because of that is a much more common Biblical occurrence.

You and I should not need an intermediary. The Urim and Thummim offers us the direct line we seek for the clearest connection possible.

Eight

RACHEL AND THE HOUSEHOLD GODS

"And Laban went to shear his sheep: and Rachel had stolen the images that were her father's." Genesis 31:19

here is a story in Genesis about Rachel stealing statues from her father, Laban. Although we do not know clearly what the statues were, it is apparent they are very valuable to Laban and he is extremely upset by their loss. They may have had significant spiritual importance.

According to scholars, these 'images,' as they were called, represented gods used in ancient divination:

"…wherefore has thou stolen my gods?" Genesis 31:30

The concept of household gods or images is mentioned 64 times in the King James Version of the Bible, particularly in later books when the destruction of these images became of great importance because they were seen as evil:

"But thus shall ye deal with them: ye shall destroy their altars, and break down their images, and cut down their groves, and burn their graven images with fire." Deuteronomy 7: 5

"And there they left their images, and David and his men burned them." II Samuel 5:21

One of the more interesting stories about the images involves David when his wife helps him escape imprisonment and certain death from Saul by placing one of them in his bed, putting a goat wool cap on it and covering it with a blanket, allowing David time to escape:

> "And when Saul sent the messengers to take David, she said, He is sick. And when the messengers were come in, behold, there was an image in the bed, with a pillow of goat's hair for his bolster," I Samuel 19:15-16

The description here implies the images were not little statues, but could have been quite large, and that description is consistent with the household gods of Laban. When Rachel took her father's gods, she covered them and sat on them, again, implying they were also fairly large:

> "Now Rachel had taken the images, and put them in the camel's furniture, and sat upon them. And Laban searched all the tent but found them not. Genesis 31:34

The next part of this story helps us understand the use of Urim in its context. Later after Saul has eighty-five priests killed, he attempts to speak to the Lord, but gets no answers:

> "And when Saul inquired of the Lord, the Lord answered him not, neither by dreams, nor by Urim, nor by prophets." I Samuel 28:6

Because he cannot get any help from the Lord through the direct communication of Urim, Saul decides to consult the 'Witch of Endor,':

> "And Saul disguised himself, and put on other raiment, and he went, and two men with him, and they came to the woman by night: And he said, I pray thee, divine unto me by the familiar spirit, and bring me him up, whom I shall name unto thee." I Samuel 28:8

After making sure she would not be punished, Saul requested that the 'witch' channel the spirit of the recently deceased Samuel, who is initially upset at being brought back from the dead. Samuel tells Saul he is out of favor with the Lord and of his impending death the following day, which happened, just as it was foretold. It is a really great story that illustrates clearly a Biblically unacceptable means of divination – the witch – and compares it with the Urim, which is reserved only for the righteous.

Some scholars speculate the Urim and Thummim may have been similar to the statues of the household gods, similar to those used by the Romans or Egyptians.

Teraphim

> "And the man Michah had a house of gods, and made and ephod, and teraphim, and consecrated one of his sons who became his priest." Judges 17:5

Another word used to describe the household gods is the Hebrew term Teraphim, meaning 'givers of prosperity,' which I believe deserves a closer look here because according to some accounts they were used for divination purposes. The word is only mentioned six times in the Bible.

According to Free Dictionary.com:

> Teraphim were consulted by the Israelites for oracular answers.

We have no clear idea of how the statues were used for divination, if indeed they actually were. A more common definition of the teraphim is the following, found in Webster's dictionary:

> Small idols representing household gods, used among ancient Semitic peoples.

While Urim and Thummim were obviously pocket sized, the statues could have come in many sizes. My interpretation of this is that the images were large statues like the Greeks and other ancients had in their homes and gardens, and the teraphim were probably smaller replicas of these used for travel, or to carry with the people for protection or as good luck talismans.

Therefore, it would make sense for some to speculate that the Urim and Thummim could have been more closely related to the teraphim, but I doubt it. Teraphim were consistently condemned beginning with the Book of Judges. Urim and Thummim were consistently clear and authorized by the Lord.

There is another amazing theory about the question of teraphim. In the 1920's and 30's a team from Harvard University excavated a site at Nuzi, a former agricultural center in the ancient kingdom of Arrapha buried under what is now modern-day Kirkuk, Iraq.

Nearly 5000 tablets were found at Nuzi, which gave archeologists and historians' clues to ancient Biblical times. The Nuzi tablets consist primarily of business and legal documents, some of which give actual proof of the existence of Abraham, Isaac and Jacob. Today they are housed in the Semitic Museum at Harvard.

Based on interpretations of the Nuzi Tablets, which were written in ancient Babylonian, some scholars believe the term 'teraphim' could actually be the equivalent of a deed to all of Laban's property. This theory actually makes sense when you read the passage because Jacob left Laban's home in secret, taking his two wives (Laban's daughters), Rachel and Leah and their children with him. Laban travels for seven days chasing them and when he finally catches up to them, he accuses Jacob of stealing everything he has:

> "And Laban said to Jacob, What hast thou done, that thou has stolen away unawares to me, and carried away my daughters, as captives taken with the sword? Wherefore didst thou flee away secretly, and steal away

from me; and didst not tell me, that I might have sent thee away with mirth, and with songs, with tabret, and with harp? And hast not suffered me to kiss my sons and my daughters? Thou hast not done foolishly in so doing." Genesis 31:26-28

Initially when reading this, you think he is upset because of the loss of his daughters and grandchildren, but soon he asks about the gods, but Jacob has no idea that Rachel stole them and tells him so, suggesting he kill whoever took them as proof of his innocence:

"With whomever thou findest thy gods let him not live: before our brethren discern thou what is thine with me, and take it to thee. For Jacob knew not that Rachel had stolen them." Genesis 31:32

This certainly suggests that whatever these images were, they were invaluable to Laban. Personally I still believe they were statues and not property deeds simply because of the later books of Judges, although of course, some of the meaning could have been lost in translation, so both theories may be correct to some extent. I do not believe they are directly connected with Urim and Thummim because they are not Biblically authorized and the terms seem to be used in entirely different contexts, implying they are not the same.

"Depart from evil, and do good; seek peace, and pursue it."

Psalm 34:14

Nine

DUALITY THEME IN THE BIBLE

ecently there was a news story you probably heard about where a plane bound to Canada from France crashed on the runway and everyone escaped unhurt. When I heard about it on the radio, I had to come home and take a look on the news to see what had happened. The paper called it a 'miracle,' and clearly it was, so why was couldn't I just feel thankful everyone was okay and leave it at that?

When was the last time you slowed down to take a closer look at a car accident? We all want to see what happened, even though it's not pleasant, and we really don't want to admit we looked, but we did, right? It's a really interesting phenomenon I think represents the darker side of our nature. There's nothing wrong with it, it's just how we are. We are creatures filled with duality and our lifetimes are spent working to balance the lighter and darker sides of our nature.

Urim and Thummim is as a binary form of divination, in other words, a tool offering a yes/no or polarizing result, just like the duality with each of us. Throughout the Bible and other ancient texts, as we'll see later in the book, duality is a major theme.

The cherubs on the Ark of the Covenant offer an example of the duality in the Bible:

> "One cherub on the end of this side, and another cherub
> on the other end on that side: out of the mercy seat..."
> Exodus 37:8

The two cherubs could represent some type of binary tool, yet it is not ever explicitly discussed. Later in the next section we will see where other cultures have used the duality offered by two beings as divinatory tools.

One of the more interesting accounts of duality is the story of Jacob and Esau in Genesis. From the moment they are conceived, there was a conflict:

> "And the children struggled within her; and she said, If it be so, why am I thus? And she went to enquire of the Lord. And the Lord said unto her, Two nations are in thy womb, and two manner of people shall be separated from thy bowels; and the one people shall be stronger than the other people; and the elder shall serve the younger." Genesis 25:22-23

This prophecy was fulfilled in Genesis 27 when their blind elderly father, Isaac, sent the oldest son Esau into the fields to hunt for him and upon his return he was to receive a great blessing which would ensure him wealth and power throughout his life.

On his mother's request and against Jacob's better judgment, he disguises himself and receives the blessing intended for his older brother. It's just one of the many Biblical encounters of duality and good vs. evil.

The character of Esau is darker, by nature, than his brother Jacob, yet in this scene Jacob engages in a deception to receive his birthright. Biblical scholars ponder this scene and its meaning and wonder if it was through God's will, or fate, that Jacob receives the blessing because he is the true chosen, regardless of how he received it.

The concept of Urim and Thummim is like a thermometer testing light against dark, right against wrong. When you use any tool of divination, you seek an answer and that answer ultimately reveals your fate.

There is an ancient set of manuscripts called the *Apocrypha* (Greek for "hidden things") containing books of the Bible that are included in the Catholic Vulgate but not accepted by Protestants because of their Greek origins. Some of these important texts are found in the Dead Sea Scrolls.

After asking the question about the potentially lost meanings of Urim and Thummim, I began to search the Apocrypha for answers.

One interesting thing I discovered were the last Testaments of each of the original sons of Israel. On their death beds, each gathered his family to his side and told them of various sins they committed in life, how the Lord granted them grace, and warnings to their offspring and family members not to follow their sinful ways.

One section that was of particular interest is the Testament of the priest Levi, which is part of the Dead Sea Scrolls. In his Testament, Levi tells his family of the day an angel of Heaven visited him and the Lord spoke to him directly:

> And thereupon the angel opened to me the gates of heaven, and I saw the holy temple, and upon a throne of glory the Most High. And He said to me: Levi, I have given thee the blessing of the priesthood until I come and sojourn in the midst of Israel. Then the angel brought me down to the earth, and gave me a shield and a sword," Testament of Levi, Chapter 2: 9-11

Another example of duality is in the following example as Judah gives his Testament to his family and recounts the family blessings:

> 29 And the Lord blessed Levi, and the Angel of the Presence, me; the powers of glory, Simeon; the heaven, Reuben; the earth, Issachar; the sea, Zebulun; the mountains, Joseph; the tabernacle, Benjamin; the luminaries, Dan; Eden, Naphtali; the sun, Gad; the moon, Asher. Testament of Judah, Chapter IV: 29

Heaven and earth, mountains and sea all offer duality also found in the Urim and Thummim. It is interesting to see the references here to the sun and moon, two important concepts in the Egyptian Priesthood and other religious systems of the world.

As we move into the next section, we will explore the possible origins of Urim and Thummim as the concept relates to other systems throughout the world as the theme of duality continues.

Part 2

DIVINATION
THROUGH THE AGES

"Teach Thy Tongue to Say 'I do not know'."

Hebrew Proverb

 Ten

URIM AND THUMMIM IN HEBREW LITERATURE

s one of the three major Abrahamic religions (Christianity, Judaism and Islam), it makes sense to consult Hebrew literature when researching Urim and Thummim.

Not surprisingly, Urim and Thummim do appear in the Tanakh, which is the Hebrew Bible. I also did an extensive search of the Qur'an, but was unable to find any references of Urim and Thummim to mention in this writing.

In the Tanakh, the term Urim and Thummim appears in the Torah, or the five collective books of Moses. The first references are in Exodus with a description of the breastplate of judgment:

> "You shall make a breastplate of decision, worked into a design; make it in the style of the ephod: make it of gold, of blue, purple and crimson yarns, and of fine twisted linen. It shall be square and doubled, a span in length and a span in width. Set in it mounted stones, in four rows of stones. The first row shall be a row of carnelian, chrysolite, and emerald, the second row: a turquoise, a sapphire, and an amethyst; the third row: a jacinth, an agate, and a crystal; and the fourth row: a beryl, a lapis lazuli and a jasper. They shall be framed with gold in their mountings." Torah Exodus 28:15-20

The Torah also reveals that there were numbers inscribed on each of the stones:

"The stones shall correspond (in number) to the names of the sons of Israel: twelve, corresponding to their names. They shall be engraved like seals, each with its name, for the twelve tribes." Torah Exodus 28:21

You may remember in the section on the breastplate in the Bible I mentioned the one theory that these stones were used as oracles and that the engravings on them would somehow light up to reveal divine information. This is what I was talking about and it is also mentioned in the Biblical version of Exodus in the same verse.

Here, as in the Bible, the design of the garments are described and the stones to rest on the priest's shoulders:

"It shall have two shoulder-pieces attached; they shall be attached at its two ends. And the decorated band that is upon it shall be made like it, of one piece with it: of gold, of blue, purple and crimson yarns, and of fine twisted linen. Then take the two lazuli stones and engrave on them the names of the sons of Israel: Six of their names on the one stone, and the names of the remaining six on the other stone, in the order of their birth. On the two stones you shall make seal engravings – the work of a lapidary – of the names of the sons of Israel. Having bordered them with frames of gold, attach the two stones to the shoulder-pieces of the ephod, as stones for remembrance of the Israelite people, whose names Aaron shall carry upon his two shoulder-pieces for remembrance before the Lord." Exodus 28:6-12

Next the Urim and Thummim is described:

"Aaron shall carry the names of the sons of Israel on the breastpiece of decision over his heart, when he enters the sanctuary, for remembrance before the Lord at all times. Inside the breastpiece of decision you shall place the Urim and Thummim, so that they are over Aaron's heart when he comes before the Lord. Thus Aaron shall carry the instrument of decision for the Israelites over his heart before the Lord at all times." Exodus 28:29-30

In this modernized version of the directions for Aaron, it suggests that both the breastplate and the Urim and Thummim are collectively called the 'instrument of decision,' and that both should be used when consulting the Lord.

Other references to Urim and Thummim correspond completely with their Biblical counterparts. Unfortunately, there are no further insights found in the Tanakh, which is basically a reflection of our own Biblical Old Testament.

Urim and Thummim at Yale

I learned an interesting historical fact about Urim and Thummim. In the late 1700's a man named Rabbi Carigal became close friends with Reverend Ezra Stiles, Yale's fifth president.

At the time, well educated colonial Christian scholars were fascinated by the ancient Hebrew language and thought that since the Old Testament is one in the same, there would be value to learn it in its original language for purposes of clarity.

Carigal taught Stiles Hebrew and he eventually became so versed in it, he translated the Hebrew Bible in to English. Stiles was elected President of Yale in 1777 and implemented the study of Hebrew into the Freshman curriculum.

Stiles commissioned a painting of his friend Rabbi Carigal, which was hung at Yale, and to this day, the school seal bears the spirit of the words Urim and Thummim through the Latin words Lux et Veritas – Light and Truth.

Secret Teachings

Because the Urim and Thummim are not mentioned more extensively within the Hebrew Bible, it caused me to refine my earlier conclusion that something was cut out of the original texts. Certainly, that is a possibility, however another possibility is that the teaching of Urim and Thummim was so sacred it was perhaps kept as an oral teaching only, or is among the lost works of the Bible, such as those texts found within the Nag Hammadi Library in upper Egypt in 1945.

I searched the thirteen codices within the Nag Hammadi but could not find any direct references to the Urim and Thummim, although that does not mean it does not exist under a name I may be unfamiliar with. I am convinced that somewhere there is evidence of the entire context and use of this most precious Biblical tool. The journey continues as we explore more possibilities in the next chapters.

Eleven

URIM AND THUMMIM DIVINE THE BOOK OF MORMON

"He said there was a book deposited, written upon gold plates...that the fullness of the everlasting Gospel was contained in it, as delivered by the Savior to the ancient inhabitants:

Also, that there were two stones in silver bows – and these stones, fastened to a breastplate, constituted what is called the Urim and Thummim...and the possession and use of these stones were what constituted Seers in ancient or former times; and that God had prepared them for the purpose of translating the book."

The Testimony of Joseph Smith

nother place where I found the Urim and Thummim to be quite prevalent was in the Book of Mormon.

Six months before I read *The Alchemist*, I began having visions of the Book of Mormon and knew I needed to get it, for some unknown reason. Shortly after that, I met my friend who I mentioned earlier, who sent me a copy of it along with lots of other information. At the time, I had no idea why I needed it until some months later when she sent me the information on the Urim and Thummim. Suddenly it all made sense, at least to some extent.

Understanding the beginnings of Mormonism is key to the study of the Urim and Thummim.

Mormonism began when founder Joseph Smith was a young Biblical student who felt confused by the numerous denominations and teachings of Christianity. He prayed to God to show him the true and correct way to practice his faith.

Smith's prayers were answered on September 21, 1823, when he was visited in his room by what he called, "A messenger sent from the presence of God," named Moroni who gave Smith specific instructions about the location of some gold plates and other items buried near his home that he would later use to translate the Book of Mormon.

Moroni told Smith the plates were hidden in a stone box on the west side of a place called Hill Cumorah, in Ontario County, New York. After the visitation, Smith visited the hill and located the gold plates and another item he called the "Urim and Thummim."

Smith was commanded to wait four years before digging up the gold plates and revealing this information to the world, and that meanwhile, he was directed to make an annual pilgrimage to the site to check on his newfound treasure.

Every September 22 from 1823-1827, Smith went to the Hill to check on the plates, and on the fourth year, in 1827, he dug them up, took them home, and began the work of translation.

Smith describes the Urim and Thummim as 'seer stones' used to assist him in translating the cryptic languages on the gold plates to English.

Witnesses said Smith tediously translated the text by peering into a hat where the Urim and Thummim would light up, revealing the English translation. This description of how the tool worked is akin to the interpretation of how some believe the stones in the breastplate lit up to reveal messages from God to the Priests in Biblical times.

The Pearl of Great Price, one of the foundational books of the Mormon religion, describes Smith's Urim and Thummim as follows:

> "There were two stones in silver bows and these stones, fastened to a breastplate, constituted what is called The Urim and Thummim. The possession and use of these stones were what constituted "seers" in ancient or former times; prepared by God for the purpose of translation."

The Book of Mormon further describes them as:

> "Two stones which were fastened into the two rims of a bow."

Since Smith's description of the Urim and Thummim differs from other scholarly theories of the stones, nobody knows for sure what they were made of, and although there were eleven witnesses who attested to the validity of the Book of Mormon at one time, none of the witnesses ever saw the stones with their own eyes, again making the identity a mystery.

Further speculation on the nature of the Urim and Thummim is documented in section 130 of the Doctrine & Covenants 130:4, where Smith asks the Lord:

> "Is not the reckoning of God's time, angel's time, prophet's time and man's time according to the planet on which they reside?"

And he receives the following answer:

> "Yes, but there are no angels who minister to this earth but those who do belong or have belonged to it. The angels do not reside on a planet like this earth; but they reside in the presence of God, on a globe like a sea of glass and fire, where all things for their glory are manifest, past, present and future and are continually

before the Lord. The place where God resides is a great Urim & Thummim. This earth in it's sanctified and immortal state will be made like unto crystal and will be a Urim and Thummim to the inhabitants who dwell theron, wherby all things pertaining to an inferior kingdom, or all kingdoms of a lower order, will be manifest to those who dwell on it, and this earth will be Christ's. Then the white stone mentioned in Revelation 2:17 will become a Urim & Thummim to each individual who receives one whereby things pertaining to a higher order of kingdoms will be made known; and a white stone is given to each of those who come into the Celestial Kingdom, whereon is a new name written, which no man knoweth save he that receiveth it. The new name is the keyword."

Doctrine & Covenants 30:5-11

The passage suggests that during the time of the second coming that man will have the ability to speak directly with God through the Urim and Thummim, without the aid of the priest. Here is the passage from the Book of Revelation:

"He that hath an ear, let him hear what the Spirit saith unto the churches; To him that overcometh will I give to eat of the hidden manna, and will give him a white stone, and in the stone a new name written, which no man knoweth saving he that receiveth it."

Revelation 2:17

I read commentary about the above verse and discovered some Biblical scholars who say that the white stone represents acceptance and the black, rejection. I searched for other references to the black and white stones in the Bible, but did not find any. It makes me wonder how the commentator reached that conclusion because there is no evidence for it.

The idea that new names will be given during the apocalypse (Greek for unveiling) is key to the Mormon faith.

Smith also received a prophecy that he was to restore the Aaronic Priesthood, the same order of Priests who wore the great breastplate in Biblical times. In order to do this, he baptized his followers in the river near his home.

Commentary on Smith's Revelation

One interesting thing about the study of the Church of Jesus Christ of Latter Day Saints is the written accounts of the languages Smith says the golden plates had on them. Among the cryptic languages were ancient Assyrian, Chaldean, Arabic and Egyptian Hieroglyphics, which were actually identified by a third party.

One of the translations of the plates is called The Book of Abraham and appears in the Mormon doctrine, The Pearl of Great Price. Here's what it says about Abraham's connection to the Urim and Thummim:

> "And I Abraham had the Urim and Thummim, which the Lord my God had given unto me, in Ur, of the Chaldees...And the Lord said unto me, by the Urim and Thummim, that Kolob was after the manner of the Lord..." Pearl of Great Price, Book of Abraham 3:1-4

After this initial reference which suggests an actual origin for the Urim and Thummim, it is mentioned several more times in the Pearl of Great Price, describing how it is used by several different people for prophecy throughout the book.

The fact that the characters on the gold plates were of ancient origins leads me to believe there is surely a connection to ancient civilizations to explore – primarily the Egyptian connection. Ever since first hearing of the Urim and Thummim, I have intuitively sensed the origins of this device are Egyptian. As we continue our look at divinatory tools and their sources, we will look into this idea in depth as the mystery of the origins of Urim and Thummim continues.

Twelve

EDGAR CAYCE SPEAKS
ON URIM AND THUMMIM

**"The holy of holies, the ephod, Urim and Thummim;
all of these were parts of the entity's experience."
T5259-001:20**

The life and work of Edgar Cayce is a major inspiration for this book. As mentioned earlier, while I was writing and researching my book on Cayce, I was unaware of what the term Urim and Thummim even meant, yet since then, I have researched the life readings and discovered he mentions this subject 46 times in 42 documents.

In one reading Cayce did for himself, he asked the Source to clarify some things about psychic ability:

> Q) What other glands in the body, if any, besides the Leydigan, pineal, and glands of reproduction, are directly connected with psychic ability?

> A) Hence these may literally be termed, that the pineal and the Leydig are the SEAT of the soul of an entity. As to the activities of physical reproduction, much of the activity of the Leydig makes for that as of embryonic in its activity, or of sterility in its activity. So we have those channels. These are not the psychic forces, please understand! They are the CHANNELS through which the activities have their impulse!

Though the manifestations may be in sight, in sound, in speech, in vision, in writing, in dreams, in Urim or Thummim, or in any. For these represent the Urim and Thummim in their essence, or in ANY of the responding forces in a body; but their impulse arises from or through these sources in much the same manner as the heart and the liver are of the physical body the motivating forces, or impulses, that carry the stream of life itself; or as the brain is that motivating center of impulse or mind. These are merely as illustrations that the student may better understand the activity of that being presented. T294-142: 3*

It is interesting to note in the previous reading that the Source speaks of the Creator's communication through dreams or Urim and Thummim – the same thing was mentioned in the Bible. He seems to be saying that the Urim and Thummim or dreams, writing, visions, or the glands mentioned by the questioner are merely the tools by which we receive higher levels of psychic or divine information.

In another reading, a woman asks Cayce about communicating with God:

Q) Is there any likelihood at the present time of developing a machine, based on the action of the electromagnetic cell, which may assist in securing direct communication as done by Aaron and Moses – and many others – with the Urim and Thummim?

A) Find in the self that as Hatshepsut put to self, in knowing who should be chosen – yet the trouble arose. Do not make the same mistake, that the VIBRATION is the force – but that which impels same from the Creative Force. Such machines are claimed to be made. Some do, some do not create the right vibration. Too oft does there enter in those personalities of those seeking. Then, in self find the way to air, and call again or Ra-Ta – and on Hatshepsut – they are as Urim and Thummim, a channel only.

T0355-001

Again, the Source is speaking of the Urim and Thummim as the tool for divine connection warning the questioner not to rely too much on that, but to realize it is to be seen as a tool for receiving the divine communication.

Another woman was told she was a daughter of Levi of the Bible and had an intimate connection to Urim and Thummim:

> "The entity then was among the daughters of Levi, and those chosen to make the vestment of the priest. And to the entity, because of its own abilities, there was given the preparation of the settings of the breastplate and the putting of the stones thereon, and the preparation of the Urim and Thummim for the interpretations of the movements that came upon the high priest in the holy of holies to be given to his people in or from the door of the tabernacle." 987-002: 6

Here Cayce mentions what we discussed earlier, that the Urim and Thummim must have been used within the Holy of Holies as a means of communicating the Creator's will to the people as he occasionally did through the door of the Tabernacle. Cayce uses the words 'interpretations of movements,' which could imply that the Urim and Thummim did not give a simple 'yes' or 'no' response, but as we already discussed, it may have many levels of communication which required the priest's insight to understand.

Another questioner came in after having a disturbing dream about his mother:

> Q)"(In the dream) I swung ma around and threw her face forward against the wall, hurting her face severely. Her face actually hurt or seemed to when she awakened."
>
> A) Well that each individual attempt to correlate those conditions as do appear in vision, or through Urim, and bring

same to consciousness, that the physical conditions may be developed and strength may be gained individually, that will assist in giving much to self's satisfaction (never self-gratification), to self's development, to self's abilities to be of service to many. TO106-008:5

Here Cayce used the term 'Urim' synonymously with 'vision' as if the information received through visions is from the same place as the divine connection with Urim. He suggests that we can learn to take the information gathered in that highest space and use it in the physical world for good.

The next reading further substantiates Cayce's use of the term by showing that the Urim and Thummim or the information obtained through dreams is more pure and therefore more valuable than other tools of expression:

Q) Can the entity's psychic faculties be expressed or developed through numerology?

A) As we have indicated oft, astrology and numerology and symbology are all but the gateways or the signs of expression. Hence intuitive force is the better, for in this there may come more the union of the spirit of truth with Creative Energy; thus the answer may be shown thee, whether in Urim, in Thummim, in dream, in numbers, in whatever manner or form. For He is the strength of them all, and beareth witness in thee and through thee if ye but do His biddings. TO261-015:22

Calling the Urim and Thummim the 'intuitive force' suggests the connection to the Creator, or as Cayce says here, the 'Creative Energy.'

On August 23, 1925, Cayce consulted the Source about dreams he was having, and the Source again speaks of Urim as though it is a connection to the divine and how Urim is used to help us with earthly lessons and knowledge:

Now, we find the body and the body-mind, and the desire of knowledge, of enquiring of forces pertaining to elements of development, are separate condition, or should be considered as such (if we) would understand in a material manner the conditions as pertain to vision, dream, or Urim, that would be made beneficial to body's desiring, wishing, to know these lessons that might be, could be, would or should be, gained from such as dreams. TO294-035:2

Cayce had another reading on April 12, 1934, discussing a dream he had about his deceased mother:

Q) Please elucidate upon the experience I had last month in New Mexico when seeing and talking with my mother, in which she materialized a silver dollar.

A) As has been given, either by vision, by prayer, by Urim, by Thummim, by dream, or in the material things, may the vision of those that are in the heart and mind of individuals given through the powers of those in the spirit plane to enter into association, communication, or activity with those that they seek to guide.

Again, the Source explained the many ways that such a spiritual connection could occur from beyond the grave, though dreams, symbols or the Urim and Thummim.

Another woman asked for guidance during her reading and was told that would come through a divine connection and acknowledgement of the Creator using any number of means, including the Urim and Thummim:

Q) Please explain and interpret the urge, which I have to engage in some constructive activity, yet cannot quite grasp the proper method or direction of procedure?

A)...God has not left His children without that promise, "As ye hold to me, I will hold to thee – If ye will be my children, I will be thy God." As He has spoken through prophet, through sage, through Urim, through Thummim, through dream, through vision, since man has been in materiality or in matter, so may the spirit of truth still five expression to those that seek His face, and to find expression of same among their fellow man.

In a reading concerning the Lapis stone, one questioner wanted to know about its value:

Q) Of what value is it?

A) Of particular value to those who are interested in things psychic! Read what was in the first effort that was made, as to all those that used the stones as settings to induce the influences from without that would aid an individual in its contact with the higher sources of activity.
(Urim & Thummim – Exodus 28:15-30) TO440-002:46

Here, Cayce suggests the stone in the second row of the breastplate is a Lapis, rather than a sapphire. In my last book, I noted the fact that Cayce was probably correct in this assumption because geological evidence suggests that Lapis would be a more commonly occurring stone than sapphires in the areas where Biblical history unfolded.

As far as his response to the questioner, he refers to the Urim and Thummim, not by name, but by describing their purpose as an instrument to help people contact higher realms.

In one reading the Source chastises the questioner for vanity and refers to the slow steady progress made by key Biblical figures:

Q) Which elements in particular would be of the greatest value to observe their effects?

A) Elements as related to that thou hast in hand, see? Dost

though hope in thine self to find in two weeks or two months that it took two men, guided by the Father Himself, eighty years to find? (Moses – Aaron – Urim and Thummim?) Thou art indeed wise, my son, but not wise in thine own conceit. As God has given, it is a doing thing to accomplish that. As may be had in thine experience to become worth while, thou mayest accomplish in forty days that as required them forty years; for thou hast an Advocate with the Father through the Christ that will guide thee, if thou wilt but put thy trust wholly in Him and not climb up some other way! TO440-016:22

Cayce also told a woman of the protective nature of Urim:

"This the presentation of that force that will guide, guard and protect, would the entity but keep in that way in which the forces may be manifest to the physical through Urim or through the visions." TO900-079:12

Like the other reading we saw earlier, in this passage, Cayce again refers to the information received from the divine and how it can be brought into the physical plane through the Urim and visions. We can use the Creator's energy to manifest things on the physical plane.

Several readings, many more than what is listed here, correlate the term Urim with the super conscious or higher self of the individual as in the following two passages:

"In the mental forces, the subconscious in its development takes hold, as it were, on such subject matter, such data, as is presented in the sleeping state, and through Urim…" T0900-090: 2

"Yet the voice through Urim, through Dream, through many, will give that information to be executed by…" TO900-151:7

Cayce described a priestly adornment worn by a woman in her

previous life – his version of a robe with Urim and Thummim:

> "The color of the robe was pearl-gray, as would be called now, with selvage woven around the neck, as well as that upon the edge, as over the shoulder and to the bottom portion of same; no belts, but those which are woven in such a manner that into the selvage portion of the bottom was woven the Thummim and Urim. These were as the balance in which judgments were passed by the priest. But these were woven, not placed upon the top of same. Neither were there jewels set in same." T3175-003:20

In summary, Cayce seemed to connect the term Urim and Thummim most frequently with the super conscious knowingness obtained in the dream state or in deep prayer like communications with the divine. If God's energy resides in the 'super conscious' plane of reality and dreams, Urim and Thummim or visions are ways we step down that energy to bring it into our own realities, then clearly Cayce supports the concept of the Urim and Thummim as tools to a clear connection to God.

*Note to readers on Cayce reference numbers: Edgar Cayce gave over 14,000 individual readings during his lifetime and these are categorized by numbers – the section numbers and the final number referring to the paragraph where the information can be found.

Thirteen

THE PENDULUM SWINGS

"The unconscious mind is decidedly simple, unaffected, straight-forward and honest. It hasn't got all of this facade, this veneer of what we call adult culture. It's rather simple, rather childish... It is direct and free." Milton Erickson, 1902-80, Father of Modern Hypnosis

ver since I can remember there has been one oracle that is my very favorite of all – the pendulum. It makes me wonder if I was a dowser in a past life because I seem to have a deep intuitive rapport with this particular tool. As you work with different oracles, I am sure you will discover a favorite of your own, if you haven't already.

A pendulum is any stone or heavy item suspended by a string or most commonly a chain that gives the user answers to yes and no questions. The rich history of the pendulum, combined with the binary or dual nature of the information it provides, makes it a logical choice to discuss here, because like Urim and Thummim, it gives binary choices.

Historically, the pendulum is an evolution of the ancient divining rods used throughout the world in ancient times. Practically every important civilization from the Egyptians, Sumerians, Greeks and so on have used some type of dowsing instruments at some point in history to locate everything from water to food to treasure. Anything man needed from the material world could be located using dowsing methods.

Proponents of dowsing like to refer to a passage in Exodus where Moses strikes a rock and commands water to flow from it:

> "And the Lord said unto Moses, Go on before the people, and take with thee of the elders of Israel; and thy rod, wherewith thou smotest the river, take in think hand, and go.

> Behold, I will stand before thee there upon the rock in Horeb; and thou shalt smite the rock, and there shall come water our of it, that the people may drink. And Moses did so in the sight of the elders of Israel."
> Exodus, 17:5-6

Critics of the 'Moses as dowser' theory site that striking a rock has absolutely nothing to do with dowsing. I report it here so you can be the judge.

As far as the pendulum is concerned, it was first written about in 1833 by French chemist Michel-Eugene Chevreul, who was asked to study the mysterious oscillations. He concluded its movements can be attributed to muscle movements directed by the subconscious mind which may be why the pendulum has continued to be linked to hypnosis, although it is rare for therapists to use it to induce trance in clients.

I've written about pendulums at length in my book *Gemstone Journeys*. As a hypnotherapist, I think this is a natural tool for me to use, and I want to spend a few moments now telling you how I think it works.

I believe we have two parts to our minds, the conscious and subconscious, and that within ourselves are the answers to everything we need to know, if we can develop enough rapport within ourselves to find the answers we seek.

When first consulting the pendulum, you have an opportunity to allow your subconscious to speak to you by programming the pendulum to tell you what kind of swing means "yes" and what kind of swing means "no."

For me, the pendulum swings clockwise if my answer is "yes," and counterclockwise when it means "no."

When I am receiving information from this higher intelligence, I know it because of the clockwise-counterclockwise motion of my pendulum.

In hypnotherapy training I learned that our own unconscious mind can also be trained to speak to us. This would be the aspect of ourselves that is not all knowing, but represents the collective intelligence of all we have learned in this lifetime on the physical plane.

I felt it would be beneficial to speak to this part of myself also, from time to time, so I trained my pendulum to move differently when I contact that unconscious part of myself. In that case, a 'yes' from my unconscious is shown by a forward-backward motion, while a 'no' would be a straight line back and forth. That way, if I ever feel it necessary to contact my more earthly self, I can differentiate the two.

One of the goals of hypnosis is to help the client get into agreement consciously, unconsciously and at the higher self level. When all three aspects of a person are in alignment, manifestation is powerful and instant. It is a good practice to check in with yourself in this way from time to time, particularly when things are going really well because it gives you confirmation you can see, and also when things aren't going well. Then you have a place to start working from to turn things around in the direction where you want to go.

Your conscious mind loves ritual and things it can see and touch and feel firsthand so the tools we use can help bridge the gap between the worldly mundane and the spiritual.

When I use a pendulum, the questions asked are usually of a very simple and relatively mundane nature. The tool gives answers at the deepest levels of what the best action would be, or what would be for highest good at that moment.

As we've discussed throughout the book, the best way to use any form of divination is to allow it to assist you in the now. The pendulum shares this with many other tools we'll discuss in this book.

There are hundreds of things you can use a pendulum for. Everything from deciding what vitamins you should or should not take today, to deciding what clothes to wear, food to eat or which movie would be best at a theater. The possibilities are endless as long as questions are stated in a 'yes' and 'no' format.

Another term for this type of divining you now see a lot in alternative healing practices is applied kinesiology, or muscle testing. In this modality, you test the strength of a muscle according to truth.

You can try this right now. Hold your thumb and index finger together as tightly as you can. Now ask a question that you know is true such as 'my name is _____ (state your name).' As you say that, attempt to pull your fingers apart, and notice the strength there.

Now to contrast, hold your thumb and index finger together again and make a false statement such as 'I live on Mars.' Notice how easily your fingers come apart when you say things that are not true? Interesting! It makes you wonder about the physical makeup of habitual liars, but I suppose that is a study for another time!

Muscle testing, as it is called, can give you the same type of information as the pendulum only without the physical tool. I personally prefer the tool, but you can try both and see for yourself.

The pendulum allows the seeker to have it one way or another, and for that reason, it helps guide you to make quick decisions for your highest good by tapping into your higher self or subconscious mind.

Next, we'll look at one of my other favorites, The Runes.

Fourteen

ODIN AND THE RAVENS

Ha'vama'l

**Wounded I hung on a wind-swept gallows
For nine long nights,
Pierced by a spear, pledged to Odin,
Offered, myself to myself
The wisest know not from whence spring
The roots of that ancient rood.**

**They gave me no bread
They gave me no mead,
I looked down;
With a loud cry
I took up runes;
From that tree I fell.**
Verses 138-139

I mentioned my love of the pendulum in the last , which remains unwavering to this day, yet from time to time I enjoy exploring other forms of divination and will often purchase books or tools and leave them on the shelf for years without ever knowing why I bought them. One of those tools is the Runes.

About 3 months ago, after having a rune set on my shelf for the past two years, I was guided to finally pull it out of its safe keeping place, and since then I have found this to be one of the most profoundly revealing forms of divination I have ever experienced.

I mentioned in the beginning of the book why I think a tool should be used to talk about the present and most immediate needs of the person using it, and the runes work very well for this purpose. You can consult them daily to give you advice or insight into the day's activities and what lies ahead and they always seem accurate to me when I take a few moments to think of what it is trying to tell me.

The Viking Runes consist of twenty five stones carved with ancient symbology. Scholars are still mystified as to the origins of the Runes, the name taken from the Gothic word "runa," which means mystery.

Mythologically, the Runes were discovered by the God Odin after much personal anguish. In the epic poem above called Ha'vama'l, Odin describes how he obtained the magical Runes after hanging for a long time in a tree.

Odin was the primary God of late Germanic and Norse mythology, and the leader of the Aesir, or Norse pantheon. As God of magic, poetry, victory and the hunt, Odin reined over the dead, the battlefield and contrarily was God of Wisdom and Life Force.

His thirst for knowledge was so great; he hung himself, as described in the above poem, and was brought back to life after nine days with greater wisdom than anyone else. Scholars believe the story of Odin's resurrection could have been an inspiration for early Christianity. It may also have inspired the Hanged Man card in the Tarot.

After researching the history of the Runes, I discovered something that I feel may have ties to the Urim and Thummim.

Legend says that Odin had two beautiful pet ravens he would send out into the world every day and each night, they would fly back to him, perch on his shoulders, and tell him everything that happened. It reminds me of the gossip columns we see today. Odin's inquiring mind wanted to know what everyone was doing!

The ravens were called Huginn (or Hugin) – meaning 'Thought' and

Muninn (or Munin) – meaning 'Memory.' Supposedly after Odin heard the goings on in the world, he would sit for long periods and contemplate the discoveries of Thought and Memory.

When I saw the spelling of the names of the two birds, I couldn't help thinking of the similarities between them and the terms Urim and Thummim. Could there be a connection there? We can only speculate.

Odin's ravens represent some kind of binary form of information gathering. When we think of the aspects of thought, which is created in the now and projected on the future, verses memory, the function of linear time which has already occurred, it seems obvious to make the comparison.

In the ancient Norse poem composed sometime between the 8th and 13th century called Grimnismal, or Ballad of Grimnir, there is a reference to the ravens:

> The whole world wide, every day,
> Fly Hugin and Munin;
> I worry lest Hugin should fall in flight,
> Yet more I fear for Munin.

In any divinatory work, we often compare things in the present, or thought, to what has already happened, memory.

That is particularly the case with the next tool we'll look at – The Tarot.

"Here's something to think about: How come you never see a headline like 'Psychic wins lottery'?"

Jay Leno (1950-)

"Last night I stayed up late playing poker with Tarot cards. I got a full house and four people died."

Steven Wright, US Comedian and actor (1955-)

Fifteen

SYMBOLISM OF THE TAROT

everal years ago, I took a two month long course on the Tarot because I was fascinated by the imagery and symbolism the cards portrayed. After two months of intense study and practice, you would think I would have been reading cards my entire career, yet for some reason, I never followed that path.

I am still a student of Tarot, even now that many years have passed, I've found there to be so many things to learn and explore with the cards, I think you could probably spend a lifetime on it and still never find all the answers.

In my studies, I recently stumbled across a book on Tarot symbolism, and speculation that certain images may be synonymous with the Biblical Urim and Thummim.

The first is in the seventh card in the Major Arcana, The Chariot, which features the charioteer with two half moons on his shoulders – one happy and the other unhappy.

When I first looked at the card, I saw this image but thought there was another in the card that seemed more closely connected to what I was seeking and that is the two sphinxes in the foreground – one black and one white – who again feature different emotions on their faces.

The other card that I noticed along the same lines was the High Priestess who is surrounded by two pillars – one black and one white. The letter B is carved in the black pillar and the letter J in the white, representing Boaz ("in him is strength") and Jachin ("he establishes") from I Kings 7:15-22:

> "And he set up the pillars in the porch of the temple: and he set up the right pillar, and called the name therof Jachin: and he set up the left pillar, and called the name therof Boaz." I Kings 7:21

During my research, I had the amazing good fortune to speak at length to Mary Greer, considered one of the world's leading authorities on the Tarot, about the possibility of a link between these images and the Urim and Thummim of the Bible.

I was amazed to discover that, according to Greer, images in the Tarot had only recently, within the past few hundred years, been altered to represent a more Egyptian theme. She told me that initially the cards were Christian in origin and were considered an acceptable "game" by Roman Catholics who used them often for entertainment, but "never for fortune telling." This certainly supports the reading I did about the Boaz and Jachin symbolism on the High Priestess card, yet it was something I had never fully considered before.

I asked her about the Urim and Thummim comparison in the modern Tarot and she said the half moon images sitting on the Charioteer's shoulders were said to have whispered in his ear, giving him advice, and therefore could be compared to the tools in the breastplate. It also sounds similar to the story of Odin's ravens, or the two cherubs perching on the Ark of the Covenant.

According to Greer, the first Tarot images showed up in the early 1400's before the Renaissance began, but after the height of the dark ages. In the 1700's the Tarot was revised to include occult images linked to the Rosicrucian and Masonic traditions.

This would mean the images I saw could not directly be linked to the Biblical Urim and Thummim because they were created later. I asked Mary if she had ever seen reference to Urim and Thummim in her research into the earliest Tarot decks and she said she had not.

That being said, it is still interesting to note that the original Tarot is Biblically oriented and that discovery is another bit of information I believe is obscured to the public for whatever reason.

I told Mary I sincerely doubt that the public at large is aware of the true origins of Tarot, and she agreed, although she and others are working to educate people, perhaps it is the image of a darker, more mystical beginning that gives our modern Tarot its appeal.

Although it is not a tool of binary divination, a term Greer introduced to me, the Tarot can be used in this way depending on the type of card reading you do.

She mentioned the three card spread and its significance. The questioner usually asks the three cards to represent past, present and future or some other trinity of information. In this way, it is not giving the person such a black and white answer, but leaves room for the middle ground.

Another Biblical scholar I spoke with mentioned his theory that the human psyche needs to find a middle ground, or resting place to just "be," and maybe there is a deeply engrained psychological reason for this to be. He mentioned the bipolar disorder and the fact that it causes people to operate in either one extreme or another with no place to stop and rest in the middle.

Fear of duality is an interesting thing to think about. I personally believe we often don't like the answer to a two sided question. Often we seek advice from an oracle and when it tells us what we don't want to hear, we tend to do it over or ignore what it tells us. There is nothing wrong with that, though, because as we'll discuss later in the book, I really feel we have choices at each and every turn of our lives and if we don't like something we do have power to change it, yet sometimes I also think there are things we all probably need to hear and let's face it – sometimes the truth hurts! It is a necessary part of

So the next time you seek advice from your Tarot or other divinatory cards, notice what kind of spread you choose. That alone can offer insight into the psyche. And I don't know about you, but I plan to spend some extra time in the future studying the amazing symbolism found in the Tarot for greater understanding of many spiritual systems throughout the world.

Next we'll look at the oldest book in the world – the Chinese Book of Changes.

Sixteen

THE OLDEST BOOK IN THE WORLD

"The I Ching does not offer itself with proofs and results; it does not vaunt itself, nor is it easy to approach. Like a part of nature, it waits until it is discovered. It offers neither facts nor power, but for lovers of self-knowledge, of wisdom -- if there be such -- it seems to be the right book. To one person its spirit appears as clear as day; to another, shadowy as twilight; to a third, dark as night. He who is not pleased by it does not have to use it, and he who is against it is not obliged to find it true. Let it go forth into the world for the benefit of those who can discern its meaning."

C. G. JUNG   Zurich, 1949

The I-Ching

everal years ago I received a wooden tube filled with fortune sticks – a modernized version of an ancient Chinese divinatory system. I pulled out my Chien Tung sticks recently to take a look at them, and for the first time it really sunk in that this very tool has been used for thousands of years by the Chinese and others throughout the world because it is a precursor to the Chinese Book of Changes, or I-Ching.

Carl Jung (1875-1961) spent several years of his life studying the amazing work of the I-Ching and in part, it helped to shape his theories surrounding synchronicity, a term he coined. The history of this sacred instrument is rich in symbolism and meaning and fascinates scholars, philosophers, and mathematicians to this day who study these ancient principles in relation to chaos theory.

The written history of I-Ching begins in ancient China, when legendary, or mythological as some would say, Emperor Fu Hsi was sitting around the fire one evening enjoying a delicious feast when he noticed patterns in the cracks on tortoise shells being cooked on the fire. He took one of the scorched shells from the fire and began to examine the lines in it, interpreting them as a powerful message from the gods. From that initial insight, the foundation of the I-Ching was formalized.

I use the term 'formalized' here because in reality, written history of this or any other oracle is only a mere fraction of what actually happened through the ages. The myth of the tortoise shell most likely evolved from a practice of throwing bones, which precedes recorded history, and is the subject of the next chapter.

Scholars initially believed the Shang Dynasty (ca.1700-1027 BC) was but a myth until oracle bones were discovered in the late 1800's by a mandarin man who received them as a prescription from his doctor who called them 'dragon's bones.' As the man looked closely at the strange remedy, he noticed they were actually tortoise shells and cattle bones with pictures on them. Recognizing their value, he decided to collect the dragon bones from all herbal remedy shops.

Later in the early 20th century, the origins of these bones were finally traced to Anyang, the location of the ancient Shang capital. Over four thousand Chinese images were found on over 100,000 pieces of oracle bones and shells.

As more knowledge was gained about the Shang Dynasty, it was determined that China's first emperor, Fu Hsi was probably not a mythological figure at all, but actually used the knowledge he received from the oracle to lead his people from a society of hunter gatherers into an agrarian age, which led to the rise of civilization in early China. This divinatory system evolved from the tortoise shells and bones to tossing marked sticks similar to my Chien Tung set, to the first book dating back to sometime around 3000 B.C., making it the oldest book in world history.

The information contained in the book was preserved as Hsi's predecessors began to utilize it and the I-Ching ultimately became a sacred doctrine of the ancient Chinese people.

The tortoise shell patterns eventually evolved into the eight Trigrams, or Pa Kau, which are linear patterns with three lines each, comprising certain forces in nature. Today, the trigrams are a critical component to the fundamental philosophy of Feng Shui.

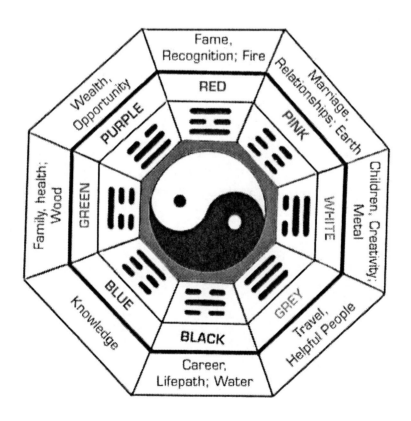

The Trigrams represent everything in the known universe: heaven or sky, earth, thunder, wind, water or moon, fire or sun, mountain and lake or marsh. Solid lines depicted strength and movement or the masculine *yang*, and broken lines represented stillness, and quiet receptiveness, or the feminine *yin*.

Two thousand years after Fu Hsi was in power, another legendary figure, King Wen decided to make some changes to the original I-Ching during his seven year incarceration in solitary confinement. One of Wen's only possessions during this time was a set of the I-Ching sticks. To keep himself occupied and entertained during his captivity, Wen decided to take the original oracle and expand it so it would be able to provide insight to more complex issues.

He did this by combining two trigrams into a hexagram with six lines each. In the new oracle, which is still in use today, there are 64 possible combinations for these lines, creating 64 hexagrams in the I-Ching system.

Many Chinese thought Wen's work to be blasphemous since the writing of any Emperor was considered divine and not to be altered, so much of Wen's writings were initially destroyed.

After his release from captivity, Wen ultimately rose to Emperor and his revisions also became sacred texts of the Chinese people. From then on, King Wen's book of writings on the subject was officially known as the 'Book of Changes,' or I-Ching, in honor of his alterations. Later, Confucius was charged with the daunting task of doing some edits to the I-Ching and created some editorial comments which were added to the Book of Changes sometime during his lifespan between 551 and 479 B.C.E..

Chinese Emperor Ch'in Shah Huang Ti (200 B.C.E.) was threatened by this wisdom and commanded Confucius' work to be destroyed. It was not until much later in 175 C.E. when one set of his writings known as the "*Ten Wings*" was considered so great they were preserved in stone so they would never be lost. Today there are two palaces dedicated to Confucius, one in his birthplace of Qufu, and the other in Beijing. Both house various stone tablets of antiquity.

Yin/Yang

My reason for including the I-Ching is not only because it is one of the world's most important writings, but because the entire text of the Book of Changes is based on Taoism, the religion of ancient China, involving the study of Yin/Yang.

The concept of Yin and Yang, I believe is key to understanding the eventual reference to Urim and Thummim in the Bible. It may very well be its original source, or one of them.

Taoist principles say the Yin (black) is the divine feminine, dark, passive, negative, and cold, and the Yang (white) is the divine masculine, light, aggressive, positive, and warm.

Taoist philosophy says that the balance of yin and yang is always in flux and changing at every moment of our lives. It is the cosmic dance, the ebb and flow of life. The Book of Changes is designed to explore the conditions within the environment of the questioner, the state of the cosmos at any given moment in regard to whatever is being asked. Like a relationship with a good friend, the I-Ching offers sound advice based on eons of human experience.

Although the I-Ching in and of itself is not a binary too, the polarity represented in the original eight trigrams represents the duality, or flux within the known universe. As in:

Heaven vs. Earth
Wind vs. Thunder
Water vs. Fire
Mountain vs. Lake

Unlike the Runes or the pendulum, or even Tarot, the I-Ching deals with major life decisions and larger energetic patterns than the mere day to day mundane existence and, in my opinion, should be used sparingly and only in matters of utmost importance.

Perhaps because it so old and has been deemed sacred for so many thousands of years, there is a certain energy you feel when preparing to consult the I-Ching – almost like a warning not to take this matter trivially – more so than with any other tool I have ever used.

When looking at systems throughout the world and making comparisons or tracing origins of Urim and Thummim, studying the I-Ching is significant because of the foundations in Taoist philosophy.

Although the Book of Changes has now expanded far beyond marks on chicken bones or tortoise shells to the 64 hexagrams, that thought reminds us that that we obviously don't understand the true origins and nature of the mystical Urim and Thummim either.

The I-Ching allows the user to take a snapshot of the issues at hand, as does the Urim and Thummim as we heard in Exodus:

> "...the Urim and Thummim; and they shall be upon Aaron's heart when he goeth in before the Lord: and Aaron shall bear the judgment for the children of Israel upon his heart before the Lord continually." Exodus 28:30

Although we've looked at this passage before, a new way to see it is to consider whether Aaron, or anyone else for that matter, truly can understand the hearts of mankind with a simple binary tool? Can we truly know our own hearts or that of our higher power through a simple yes or no? It may be that the Urim and Thummim is a far more telling tool than what we can imagine. "

"I cannot teach you how to pray in words. God listens not to your words save when He Himself utters them through your lips."

Kahlil Gibran,
"The Prophet"

Seventeen

DIVINATION IN
SHAMANISTIC CULTURES

Stones In The South Pacific

My very first book, *Origins of Huna* explored some of the customs of the Hawaiian kahunas. Ancient Hawaiians, like many other indigenous cultures, worshiped gods they called their Aumakua, which were the spirits of their deceased ancestors who they turned to for guidance and power.

Aumakua manifest themselves in the natural world including stones, which are considered sacred. On the island of Hawaii there are special stones that are said to be birth stones that supposedly grow from tiny pebbles into large rocks and will 'give birth' themselves when they are watered regularly. During special ceremonies, these rocks were part of the festivities and placed in a prominent space and called upon for wisdom and insight.

In the Tonga, custom says if black and white coral pebbles are buried together, they will increase.

According to Abraham Fornander, the world's foremost authority on Polynesian history and shamanism, there were stones used as a binary form of divination. If someone wanted to steal someone's property, he or she would consult the kahunas and stones were consulted. The questioner was asked to choose some stones from a pile of about 50. The stones selected represented the questioner and the ones left over represented the victim of the 'crime.' If the thief took an odd number of stones and left an even number behind, the venture would be successful, but if he took an even number and left an odd number behind, it was considered unlucky and unwise to pursue. If both sides received odd or even, that was also considered unlucky and the pursuit should be avoided.

Here we see a version of binary divination and the use of the black and white again. Although I have always said there are many things in each indigenous culture that we will never truly understand unless we live among the people. Many cultural practices are kept secret and only some are leaked out to the Western world.

Australian Aboriginees

The ancient aborigines have always been considered to be one of the most divinely connected populations on earth. Their innate rapport with the natural world is astounding, and as we take a look at some of the customs there, we can see a connection to the polarity in divinatory tools also used by other civilizations.

Crystals played an important role in the cosmology of the Aboriginees and one of the primary gods, Baime, who was considered 'Father Sky.' His wife, Kurikita, was completely covered in quartz crystals so whenever she moved, she lit up the sky. Her powerful husband had two crystals that rested on his shoulders and extend up to the sky. When he appears to the Aborigines in dreamtime, he provides a bridge between their life on earth and the heavens.

The reference to these stones sitting on the shoulders is reminiscent of the stones on the priest's shoulders in Exodus that also, according to some, provided divinatory information.

Unlike many systems where the sun is seen as masculine, in the Aboriginal culture, the moon is male and the man in the moon, Kidili, causes women to get pregnant. Legend tells of the female sun goddess, Gnowee, whose son got lost and was never found so she wanders every day across the sky carrying a torch to search for him.

Peru

One of my favorite places in the world is Cusco, Peru, cradle of the once great Incan civilization. I recently visited this incredible place. Most visitors are attracted to Maccu Piccu (translated means 'old mountain') which, to this day, remains one of the greatest ancient ruins and spiritual sites in the world.

There are several theories surrounding this magnificent place. One is that the ruins housed the working class citizens while rulers lived in the nearby city of Cusco, located only 112 kilometers away.

Another is that prior to the Spanish invaders capture and destruction of the Incan Empire in the 1500's, Incan rulers wisely hid the women in Maccu Piccu so they would be safe from conquerors. This theory is substantiated by the large number of female remains discovered in this area.

Others believe the city was entirely unknown to the Incas and that it predates them, although I find this hard to believe because when you go there, you can travel by train, like I did, through the stunning sacred valley where other less spectacular ruins can be found. It suggests to me that in ancient times, just like today, pilgrims made the journey back and forth between the two locations on the Inca Trail.

One of my Peruvian friends told me about this once polytheistic culture and how they worshiped the sun, gave sacrifices to the gods, and performed acts of divination by studying the lungs of llamas, a practice similar to heptoscopy, which we will discuss in a moment, performed in other parts of the world. When visiting Maccu Piccu, it is clear the ancient people had a great knowledge of astronomy and the universe because of the astronomically aligned sacred temples included within the structure. Duality was evident through the male god of creation, Viracocha and his wife, Kilya, the goddess of the Moon and fertility, a concept similar to others throughout the world.

One of the most mysterious places in Peru is the area called Nazca in the Pampa region which is a flat arid area of fields that has some amazing markings there similar to crop circles but with different designs. Mysterious stones were recovered from the region, as well, with unusual pictures on them that seem to relay detailed medical procedures and maps of the ancient civilizations Atlantis and Lemuria. Nobody knows for sure where the stones came or what they represent.

Heptoscopy in the ancient world

In the ancient world, there were several common types of divination used including the ancient art of Heptoscopy, or reading livers, which was used as early as Babylonian times, and has also been evidenced in ancient Rome.

The liver was seen as the seat of the soul and for this reason the art of liver divining became an important part of ancient culture. Archaeologists have actually uncovered evidence of this through charts showing the liver and the different interpretations of predictions obtained from them. Ancient cuneiform texts also documented this practice.

The liver is mentioned over forty times in the King James Version of the Bible and for that reason it is believed heptoscopy was practiced by ancient Hebrews. The following is just one example:

"For the king of Babylon stood at the parting of the way, at the head of the two ways, to use divination: he made his arrows bright, he consulted with images, he looked in the liver." Ezekiel 21:21

When reading the liver, markings on the right were seen as fortunate, while those on the left were unlucky. It was a complex process which at times involved other organs as well and seems to be common practice throughout the Middle Eastern region.

Africa

In Africa, the practice of divination through throwing bones has been and still is used by tribes for everything from predicting crop growth, to inquiring about the outcome of the hunt, to health reasons. The shaman will interpret and give readings based on the way the bones fall. Some scholars who studied the Urim and Thummim suggested it is a form of lots that could have been derived from this early divination practice or is similar to the act of throwing dice in ancient Greece, which we will discuss a bit further in the next chapter.

Native American Fetishes

The Zuni people are well known for carving fetishes from stone and this practice dates back to the creation myth where the twin sons of the Sun God struck some animals with lightning to keep them from harming humans. It is believed that the spirits of these animals are still alive within the stones they carve and the animal medicine can be tapped into by carrying them around.

On a trip to Alaska several years ago, my family acquired a carved ivory fetish made by the Eskimo Intuit tribe. The Inuits are among the only peoples in the world who are legally allowed to use ivory from walruses used for food to carve things from. This particular carving is of a little man said to bring luck to the user.

This practice is similar to the concept of household gods and images we looked at earlier, and somehow could be an offshoot of this very ancient practice.

Throughout the history of the world, man has held common beliefs and practices when it comes to the unseen world. Amazingly, regardless of what part of the world we look at, similarities are striking and it brings a new sense of just how connected we all really are.

Ozymandias
Greek for 'Ramses II'

I met a traveller from an antique land
Who said: "Two vast and trunkless legs of stone
Stand in the desert. Near them on the sand,
Half sunk, a shattered visage lies, whose frown
And wrinkled lip and sneer of cold command
Tell that its sculptor well those passions read
Which yet survive, stamped on these lifeless things,
The hand that mocked them and the heart that fed.
And on the pedestal these words appear:
`My name is Ozymandias, King of Kings:
Look on my works, ye mighty, and despair!'
Nothing beside remains. Round the decay
Of that colossal wreck, boundless and bare,
The lone and level sands stretch far away.

- Percy Blythe Shelley

Eighteen

URIM AND THUMMIM
IN ANCIENT EGYPT

rom the start of this project I have intuitively felt that the source or answer about what and how Urim and Thummim actually work would be found within the ancient Egyptian civilization.

It makes sense because the entire foundation of the Bible is based on the Exodus from Egypt to Israel, and the depths of Egyptian influence on all civilizations since then cannot be underestimated, although it is not always clearly documented.

If you've had the chance to read the amazing book *Secret Teachings of All Ages* by Manly P. Hall, he tells about the Urim and Thummim and the potential connection it has to high priests in the ancient Egyptian metropolis of Memphis. These priests also wore a breastplate adorned with stones and it would be easy to see how Moses could have been directed to make a breastplate similar to the ones he saw his Egyptian counterparts using.

On that same line, many scholars have speculated that Moses himself was a highly skilled adept of the Egyptian mystery schools based on his name, which Hall supposes is a derivative of an ancient term referring to solar activity.

Thoth/Hermes

I briefly mentioned in the last chapter about the ancient process of throwing dice or knucklebones in both Africa and ancient Greece. This form of divination was supposedly invented by Thoth the Atlantean, who is the Greek god Hermes, and the Roman god Mercury.

A common opinion among scholars is that the process of consulting the Urim and Thummim is merely an offshoot of the dice.

Akenaten/Amenhotep IV

I must mention the significance of the god Akenaten, who had also been called Amenhotep IV, who was husband to the most beautiful woman in the world, Nefertiti.

Raised in the polytheistic Egyptian culture, Amenhotep suddenly changed his name to Akenaten and converted the pagan culture to a monotheistic culture. Some say this was due to some divine inspiration or influence of the Israelites, or his supposed friendship with the Biblical Moses. Speculation abounds regarding this extraordinary ruler who did not look like the other people in the society. some have suggested they were from another planet, because of his and his wife's strange looks and rather large craniums, Other more secular philosophers suggest they were just from another geographical region. Nefertiti was probably also Akenaten's sister as well as his wife because her skull was also unusually formed.

There is a very famous sculpture of Akenaten in the Egyptian National Museum in Cairo called *Akenaten and his Family Offering to the Aten* carved in alabaster depicting the self proclaimed god Akenaten and his family raising their hands up to the sun as the beams of light hit them. In their hands, they hold rounded objects that seem to be illuminated by the sun. These are interpreted by museum officials as libations of some kind.

I wonder if this is some version of Urim and Thummim – objects that when held up for the Creator are illuminated with His presence and wisdom.

The coincidences surrounding the unusual and controversial way this pharaoh chose to live his life seem to suggest there is some kind of connection there.

Cayce's Ra –Ta

Even Edgar Cayce mentions Ra-Ta and Hatshepsut in one of the life readings where Urim and Thummim are discussed. The ancient Egyptians often combined names of the gods and made sub gods out of them. In the Thebes region, Ra was his only name, although in the West Delta region, there was a god named Mando-Ra. To me, I am convinced Cayce was merely speaking of another of the many incarnations of Ra, and it is reasonable to think that such practice as the use of an Urim and Thummim type tool would have been used long before the reign of Akenaten, so there could be a connection here, although we will never know for certain, at least not until the Hall of Records resurfaces, and what a glorious day that will be!

Maat vs. the Heart

If you look at Egyptian papyrus drawings, one of my favorites, and the one I got a copy of when I was there, is representation of the journey of the soul into the afterlife. The newly deceased is led in procession past several Egyptian Gods until he or she arrives at the scale where the heart is weighed against the feather of truth, represented by the goddess Maat.

There is something about this image that reminds me of the Urim and Thummim. The idea of 'lights' and 'perfections' is similar in some ways to what is being considered when the dead take their final journey.

If the person is pure and has lived a godly life, his heart will weigh the same as the feather, achieving balance, and he will go on to meet Orisis, the guardian of the dead, who is represented by some scholars as Jehovah himself. Then he or she will successfully ascend in to the afterlife.

The Khemetic religion worships Maat – truth, what is right and just in the world. If Urim and Thummim are the Hebrew version of a divine encounter, hearing the thoughts of the Creator, not in the afterlife, but while living and breathing, I believe there is some connection here.

Isis Cult and Mystery Schools

There are many who believe Moses and Jesus were seasoned adepts of the mystery schools of antiquity and today there are groups devoted to the worship of the goddess, or Isis, as she is called in her Egyptian manifestation. There is reason to believe that there were many fantastical magical workings going on in these groups that still go on today and that somewhere in those teachings and those of any number of the various mystery schools, that all kinds of divination tools were used to create divine connection.

We know that Isis' son Horus wears a double crown of Upper and Lower Egypt with a plate of gold around the mitre, which is described in the book of Exodus:

> "And thou shalt make a plate of pure gold, and grave upon it like the engravings of a signet, Holiness to the Lord. And thou shalt put it on a blue lace, that it may be upon the mitre; upon the forefront of the mitre it shall be." Exodus 28:36-37

One mystery school ritual involving Isis helped the aspirant with interpretations of dreams for divination. The person would take a piece of white linen and write the name of the god to be invoked and a black cloth representing the eye of Isis was wrapped around their hand before sleep. The chosen god would appear in the dream state and answer the questions asked, often using symbology which would later have to be interpreted.

Although there is no concrete evidence to suggest Urim and Thummim to be an Egyptian concept, it makes sense that it would be so. As one of the most formidable civilizations known to man, the influence

Egypt still has on us today is amazing. The connections to Biblical characters is also being continually debated as scholars search to piece together the puzzle that once held all of mankind together as one. In the next section you will see how connecting energetically with this ancient land can help us connect to the wisdom of the ages.

ISIS and HORUS

"The average man prays to God with his mind only, not with all the fervor of his heart. Such prayers are too weak to bring any response."

Parmahansa Yogananda

Part 3

ANSWERS FROM ABOVE

"Reality is merely an illusion,
albeit a very persistent one."
Albert Einstein

Nineteen

DIVINATION IN THE QUANTUM FIELD

bout a year ago, I released my book called *Beyond Reality: Evidence of Parallel Universes* where I explored the ideas now permeating our consciousness about quantum physics and the true nature of reality.

As we discuss the subject of divination, I would be remiss to not mention a few of my thoughts on how divination connects us to the universe.

In this book, we explored several *binary* divination tools, which is an important concept for us all to understand because the binary system suggests a tool that gives a yes or no answer, or deals in polar opposites such as black and white, hot and cold, etc.

The reason this relates to parallel realities is because of the power of choice. When you choose to consult an oracle and as it a 'yes' or 'no' question, each of the answers contains a totally different reality, if you think of it.

Let's say you want to buy a new automobile. You consult your tool of choice and ask, "Should I buy this car?" or a better way to phrase it would be, "Is it in my best interest to buy this car?"

Assuming you take the advice of the oracle, if it tells you 'yes,' then suddenly the old clunker you were driving around in gets traded in for the new model. That is one reality. You move forward from then on driving the new car, attracting the attention of all your friends and all is well.

On the other hand, if the oracle says 'no,' and you agree, you continue to drive your ten year old car, you may decide to rebuild the engine. At some point down the road in this new reality, you may lose your job and feel thankful you didn't add to your overhead by purchasing a new vehicle. Now you are experiencing this reality.

See how powerful this really is? It's as if all possibilities are sitting dormant out there in cyberspace waiting to happen, or not. And the question remains as to whether or not they both actually exist, or if they are just among the realm of possibilities.

I have enjoyed many mind-bending discussions of this very concept with a dear friend of mine who is a Catholic priest and scholar. He told me that the Catholic faith has now accepted a term used by the great scholar Thomas Aquinas called "futurables."

The question was raised as to whether or not God knows about all outcomes that did not happen but could have. The accepted answer by the church is yes; God does know all of these things and sees them as things that might have happened, as opposed to actuality.

My friend and I then batted around the very thing you and I are talking about now. What is the true nature of our Creator? Is God an all knowing force connecting everything that has, will, or could have happened? Is everything actually existing all at once? I think it seems likely, although as I tell my students, I do not believe it is for us to truly know the mind of God. How could we? Even science is made up by man!

If we did know the answers, wouldn't this be a boring place to be? The quest is the challenge and the fun, I think.

So assuming that anything you ask an oracle will create a parallel universe in the quantum field, why ask at all? Why not just go out into each of the possibilities and think it through enough to see for yourself what the outcome would be?

This is the type of work I do with people in private session all the time. I began my career as a past-life regression therapist and moved into mainly working in futures. People come to me because they feel stuck in the now. They cannot decide what is best. After going into a mild state of relaxation, I have them travel "forward" (if that even exists!) in time to see a fork in the road where they have two choices. They can do this, or they can do that. I guide them into both scenarios so they can see for themselves what would happen in each instance. Amazingly, they are able to clearly see which choice is "best."

To label the choice as better than another really isn't correct thinking either, in my opinion. We are the ones who sit around judging everything, but I doubt God judges us that harshly. I believe it comes down to the choice of what we would like to experience. Sure, some things are "easier" than others, but sometimes we pick the tough road because the lessons we learn there are greater in the long run.

Past Lives and the Nature of Time

A quick note on the concept of "past lives." I don't think they exist. Not that I don't believe we've lived before, that I am not sure of. What I mean is that I believe there is no such thing as the past. It is something we made up.

This whole idea of linear time is something we devised to get by in the world we live in, yet if Einstein's work means anything, we know time isn't real!

Einstein taught us about relativity which says that I cannot really get in your head and see how you are experiencing your life. You may think time is flying and I may think things are going at a snail's pace. This tells us that there is no such thing as time as we know it.

It makes the "futuables" concept very valid.

You are a Time Traveler

To show you how powerful you really are, do something for me now. I want you to quickly imagine it is next Thursday and you are eating lunch. Take a minute to imagine it.

Now that you've thought of it, what occurred to you? Were you in the office cramming a sandwich down your mouth as you finished that overdue report? Did you go home and catch your favorite soap opera? Did you meet your best friend for lunch at a favorite restaurant?

I would be willing to bet that you did imagine something, right? If you did, you have now seen how you willfully traveled into the future! You went to a future event, saw it, and if physicists are correct, you are more likely to create that reality than any other because you put your attention on it. Interesting, isn't it?

So the next time you consult your oracle, or any of the divinatory tools we've explored in this book, remember you can take a peek into your future at any time and see for yourself what you want to experience and go for it!

What we will share a tool and some techniques to help if you need a bit of a nudge with this automatic knowingness, like we all do from time to time, in the next chapters.

 Twenty

HOW DIVINE

Knowing this, O son of Pandu,
You will no more
Fall into such delusion;
For through this you
Will see all beings
In you Self and also in Me.

Bhagavad-Gita Verse 35

The next thing we should explore is why people turn to prophecy in the first place. In the last chapter, you saw how powerful your mind really is and how you are perfectly able to tap into the past, present and future just by thinking about them.

So why would you need a tool in the first place? I believe it's because in a three dimensional world, our minds sometimes still need three dimensional evidence of what we already know. That is, something to see, touch, feel and experience. In reality, though, you don't need any of these things at all, as you saw in the last chapter. You can easily tap into your inner knowingness to get the answers you seek.

Through the ages, human beings have always used tools of divination for a wide variety of purposes – to forecast crop growth, to serve as protection or warnings in battle, to find true love, just to name a few.

As you saw earlier in the book, everything from bones and shells, to cards to tea leaves to signs in nature have been used by man to attempt to predict the outcomes of life and to avoid catastrophe.

Deep within our subconscious we hold the keys to many things including the knowingness of the all that is, all that has been and all that could be.

It is our conscious minds that often stand in the way of true divine communication. Aside from our desire to see and touch things, divination tools are helpful for getting the ego out of the way in order to experience a clearer connection to God.

I believe we are guided by higher beings, a God-like or creative force, and/or our own higher selves or future versions of our self who travel back through time to assist us in simple daily living and if we can somehow open up lines of communication with this higher intelligence, our lives suddenly become much easier and serendipitous. As we talked about earlier, it's about listening to the possibilities then selecting the choice that takes us to the highest ground.

The subject of divination is a tricky one because in life, all things are possible. It is a dangerous game to think that a tool can run your life, or that the information received from an oracle is engraved in stone.

Caution must be used when working with any divinatory tool – caution and respect. First and foremost, you have to realize that you and only you have the power to create anything you want to create in life and knowing that, you can allow the tool to work with you, step by step, to create the life you want to live.

Life is like an eternal loop. I am convinced our concept of linear time is not valid and that all time – past, present and future – are happening all at once, right now. The only way to begin to create what you want is to be aware right now and make a decision at this moment as to what the next best step would be for you. That's where some tools are seemingly simpler than others.

Any intuitive advice, whether it's from a tool or from a psychic, is only as good as that moment and the information at hand. To me, when you seek such council, the reader is only able to tell you what they see, at that time, if everything stays as is, then such and such is likely to happen. At any moment, though, things can change and life can swing off in a new direction.

Quieting the mind, listening to that higher source of wisdom and using a tool to make that voice heard louder, at a deeper level, is the function of any tool of divination.

As you've seen for yourself in the previous chapter, life is unfolding with each and every choice we make, moment by moment. It is not always possible to forecast the future with any great reliability. The tools should be used to guide the moment we are in and not the overall outcome of our very existence, with the exception of tools like the I-Ching which don't give direct answers at all, but allow you to make choices yourself based on the energy surrounding your question.

People are constantly searching for greater meaning in their lives, wondering what their life or soul purpose is, and in private practice I hear people all the time tell me that their greatest purpose is their job. The problem with that is that we are not our jobs; we are so much more than that!

Our highest purpose in life is unfolding with each moment we live, with each breath we take and with each choice we make. It's really that simple!

I think we enjoy divination because most human beings truly want to do their best, be good people, and strive to reach a higher ground. Otherwise, we wouldn't even bother trying to connect with our Creator.

When used conscientiously and respectfully, divination tools can assist us in strengthening the connection to our own highest potential so anything becomes possible.

In the next chapter, we'll work with a tool to help you reach that potential.

"Take these," said the old man holding out a white stone and a black stone that had been embedded at the center of the breastplate. "They are called Urim and Thummim."

From *The Alchemist*
by Paulo Coelho

Twenty-One

REDISCOVERING THE ORACLE

n the next section I'm going to share some information with you about how you can create an oracle similar to Urim and Thummim, a modern version that is, and use it in your own daily life.

As you've seen the Urim and Thummim of Biblical times was something only consulted by a chosen few – the priests. I'm guided that in this ever-expanding Age of Aquarius, that it is time to reconnect with the essence of this instrument and use it right now, for all people, to make our lives a daily divine connection with the Source.

There is a certain allegorical aspect to the stories in the Bible, and I truly feel that we are all connected to the Creator and are therefore authorized to use any tool, which strengthens that bond. The Urim and Thummim provides a means of doing just that.

The nature of what you're about to discover is very similar to the systems you've been reading about in that it can be used to ask questions about the here and now, but it can also assist you in accessing the bigger picture too.

The materials revealed

Despite my exposure to the Mormon version of the Urim and Thummim and other speculations on the identity and physical appearance of the materials, I believed these stones were like yin and yang, and that I was looking for a material that was black and white in appearance, although initially I did my mortal best to let go of that expectation and allow myself to be guided to whatever material would be most beneficial for all concerned.

I began to receive messages in meditation about the time frame in which I would receive these new materials and was 'told' intuitively they were new to me, a fact that surprised me greatly, considering I was already so familiar with much of the mineral kingdom.

I was guided that I would somehow discover them on a road trip/book tour through the southwest, so initially I thought the source of the material would be in New Mexico.

Before I ever reached Albuquerque, I went to a large event in Denver, Colorado, and was struck more than ever by the great number of Egyptian displays there. I began to walk up to several of the booths and started to pick up items there and feel them with my hands.

At one point, I picked up a large scarab beetle and held it for a moment when a rush came over me and I knew this material was close to what I was looking for, but not quite it.

I inquired about the material to the vendor who told me this beetle was made of man made resin and cast at their location. It was only a simulation of the carved stone beetles.

On the second to last day of the show, I was away from my booth and when I returned, my helper told me a woman had come by to see me and she was very interested in my book *Edgar Cayce's Guide to Gemstones, Minerals, Metals & More*. He felt I should go see her and give her a copy of my book and told me it was an important connection for me.

Time went on and I was busy and completely forgot about the whole thing until the next morning when I arrived early and decided to walk around and see what other things were at the show. As I walked down one particular isle, a visual image of a number flashed through my mind and I saw the piece of paper where the woman's booth number had been written down the day before. It was 108, which is serendipitous to me because I always receive signs and omens in numbers and the number 9 is a significant one for me.

I quickly realized I was about to reach her booth, introduced myself, and immediately understood why this meeting was so auspicious. Her life's work was to procure unusual pieces from Egypt.

Once again, I walked into her booth and began to feel different objects. I reached out to pick up a black simply marked scarab and felt a powerful rush through my body. I thought, "This is it!"

I started to ask her what material it was made of, because it was something I had never seen before, even during my own journey to Egypt some years earlier. I reached it out to her without speaking and she answered before I could ask. "It's Basalt," she said, "And that one is for you. Take it."

The overwhelming rush of thoughts poured through me and I felt immense gratitude and awe that the discovery of this material had come so easily. The Urim was to be of black Basalt.

I felt around to the other beetles in the booth knowing there must be a white material to be used for the Thummim. I reached out and touched many of the beautifully carved soapstone beetles, and since this was a form of alabaster, my initial impression of what the material should be, I knew that was it!

Some time after returning from my trip, I was finally guided the time was right to begin working with the Urim and Thummim. The problem was, I still felt something was not right. I was attempting to use them in the same way they were presented in *The Alchemist* – where black is yes, and no is white. I soon realized in this system the opposite is true.

I picked up the scarab beetles and held the alabaster one in one hand, the basalt in the other, holding the thought in my mind about the new intention for them – white yes, and black no. There was suddenly a compatibility there I did not experience at first. Yin and Yang. Balance. This was it!

I shifted them and held them both with one hand, rubbed them together and continued to feel the rapport between them.

Next, I would have to discover how to use them at long last.

How to use the Urim and Thummim

This is the part you have undoubtedly been waiting for -the chance to use this new and powerful tool – Urim and Thummim.

First, when you get your set of scarabs, one of soapstone/alabaster and the other of black basalt, I want you to hold them in your hands. The best way to do this is to hold the white one in your right hand because it represents the masculine aggressive energy within your field. Put the black one in your left hand. The left side is your receptive feminine side. Within every person, male or female, are both energies, just as we discussed in the Yin and Yang section of the book. The two aspects to your energy are in continuous flux. Sometimes you need to be aggressive and assert yourself, while other times you can relax, enjoy an art exhibit and the lighter side of your nature. It's all about balance!

Hold the stones as described and I want you to become really conscious of your right hand. Feel the white scarab in it. How does it feel? Begin to say the word 'yes,' over and over again while thinking of that stone. Do this for a minute or so – as long as you feel guided – then move on to the next.
Feel the black basalt beetle in your left hand. How does that feel? Begin to say the word 'no,' over and over again while you hold it in your hand. Good.

Now alternate saying this. Think of your right hand and the white beetle and say, 'yes,' and then think of the left hand and the black beetle and say, 'no." Say it faster and faster "yes, no, yes, no…" and so on, really getting the feeling for the two energies. Great! Now you have programmed your tool by connecting with them energetically on the physical plane as well as through your higher self.

Consulting the Oracle

In the Bible, Urim and Thummim were only consulted by priests in dire need of divine direction. This was not a tool that was used for trivial things nor should it be taken lightly.

As we saw by examining so many kinds of tools from all over the world, some of them really do work differently than others. The pendulum and runes can be consulted regularly as a thermometer of minute by minute progress toward an outcome. The I-Ching, though, is much more serious and should only be consulted in times of great need and about much bigger picture things.

I think of Urim and Thummim as something in between these two extremes. Of course on the one hand, you don't ever want to become dependent on any tool, even those used daily. As we already discussed, you have the answers within you right now. You really don't need the tool at all. It is just there to help the subconscious connect with the higher power in a more visible way.

Urim and Thummim can be used daily, if you'd like, weekly, or monthly, depending on your needs. Sometimes during crisis modes, we need the aid of a tool to help get us through difficult times. It's perfectly okay to consult these things when needed – that's why we have them!

Now that you've successfully programmed your Urim and Thummim as 'yes' and 'no,' you are ready to have a consultation.

I would suggest you get a bag or some kind of container to keep them in. I like to use a little velvet pouch like the ones I carry my other stones in. Assuming your Urim and Thummim are safely tucked away in their container, you are now ready to receive the information they can provide you.

Begin by thinking about the question you want to ask. For example: Should I buy a new car?

Take a deep breath and reach into the bag and pull out one of your beetles. Notice which you received – the black, meaning 'no,' or the white, meaning 'yes.' Maybe you need more clarity than this alone, so continue asking questions until you get the answer you need to understand the situation completely.

Let's say it says 'yes,' but you need to know more such as when you should buy it. Put the stones back in your bag and inquire again. You could ask it something like this: "Should I get it this month?"

Wait for the response and continue until the issue is clear. One important thing I want you to practice is this: when you ask the initial question, stop and pay attention to any thoughts that enter your head. For example, let's say you ask about the car and suddenly a silver one pops in your head, or you see a calendar that says 'August,' or whatever. Start to pay attention to these 'thoughts' and any feelings you have because this is the elaboration on the question you asked. This is probably how, even in Biblical times, the tools 'spoke' to man. You can do this right now because you are much more tuned into this stuff than you probably even realize!

We are all so busy with our lives and bombarded with technology that it is sometimes difficult for us to stop and listen to what is being told to us at the highest levels. So allow this to be an opportunity for your growth in that area. Believe me, we can all use it – myself included!
That way, you have expanded what the tool can do for you and over time the initial response will be all you need because you will see the action plan in your mind. Like the things we discussed in the quantum physics chapter, you are traveling through time unconsciously so bring

it to your attention and see how clear your path will become!

Continue to work with it, and as always, let me remind you that there is no right or wrong with anything you are doing! You know at each moment what you should be doing and if you feel the directions above are not quite right for you, change them!

I like to call myself 'the teacher who doesn't teach,' because I want to show you how I do it, then I want you to take the best, leave the rest and do what you feel intuitively is right for you. I have all the confidence in the world that you are going to do a great job!

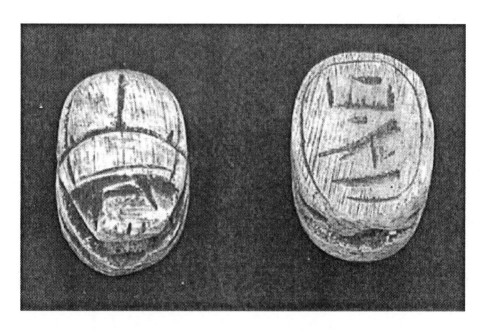

Top of Scarab   **Bottom of Scarab**

"Over the past few years in particular, modern man is receiving more answers to questions of epoch importance. The shroud of darkness and secrecy we were once under has now lifted to reveal many of the mysteries of our world."

Conclusion

he question we should ask ourselves when consulting any oracle is 'who are we trying to reach, and for what purpose?' Are we contacting a deeper knowing within ourselves, or a higher intelligence 'outside' ourselves?

Physicists would say it's one in the same – a future you reaching out to lend a hand. New Age followers should say it's a guide, angel or perhaps a loved one who's crossed to the other side.

Regardless of who or what is helping, the fact that these exercises give our human three-dimensional selves something tangible to grasp in an ever-changing and unknown universe may be reason enough to praise any tool. Any method is a Godsend, if we can continue as a species to understand ourselves and our neighbors better with less judgment.

As far as Biblical tools are concerned, much of this book has been speculation on whether or not the Urim and Thummim actually relate at all to other systems of divination from around the globe.

I'd like to think that all things had an origin somewhere in linear time and space - a place from which everything as we now know it all began. As a collective species of humankind, perhaps we are all more connected than what we ever imagined.

Any ideas or thoughts designed with unity and equality in mind are always good to promote as we work to build a world with greater tolerance and understanding of all belief systems. I truly believe they are all interpretations of the same universal truth – the divine within every living being, uniquely expressing themselves on the physical plane.

Consciously, we may never know the 'proven' answers to questions we ask, but on an intuitive level the knowingness of the soul is boundless.

Based on this research, I am definitely led to believe that Urim and Thummim were more than a mere tool of binary divination and provided its users with more than simple yes and no answers. I believe it was like having a daily link to the Holy of Holies and that it may have communicated through the spoken word to the priest, not necessarily in actual audible words, but the internal words of the spirit. It was a tool of great wisdom and insight.

What remains are the mystery about what I believe is the lost text in Exodus and other books where Urim and Thummim are mentioned. Surely there once existed a further explanation of the divination tool of God, yet at this point, we are unable to find it on the physical plane, and it remains deep within the collective consciousness.

Through that intuitive knowingness of this greatest of all oracles, we can revitalize it and use it once again in our lives to bring clarity, purpose and direction.

Do we actually need a tool to communicate with our Creator? Probably not, but as we continue our journey on earth, we are likely to continue the quest to develop stronger means of divine connection and divination is the likely road we will choose.

Over the past few years in particular, modern man is receiving more answers to questions of epoch importance. The shroud of darkness and secrecy we were once under has now lifted to reveal many of the mysteries of our world.

From the moment the Berlin Wall fell in 1989 to now, we have seen so many changes in such a short chronological time, it is amazing to think how far we've come. Little by little, the hidden aspects of all areas of life are coming to light in this most amazing Age of Aquarius.

On some level this research seems to have led to a dead end. There is no place I can find that says for certain what the tools called Urim and Thummim really are. Because I enjoy seeking the tangible proof, this project has been somewhat frustrating, yet because so much has been explored, I feel I have a deeper understanding of the ancient world than before. The humbling truth of it is that the more I learn, the more I realize I need to learn.

The scientific method man has created has somewhat enslaved the population who must adhere to strict guidelines of what is and is not acceptable proof. I hope we will learn to develop the inner knowing of the soul as a measure of proof, and when that is properly acknowledged, the outer world will know what I already do, that my research and inner speculation into this mystery is valid.

So with that, the adventure continues. I hope this writing has offered a peek under the veil and I challenge you to continue your search, as I will, to seek and learn and grow in peace, unity and tolerance of all beings. May this tool, the Urim and Thummim give you light and create perfection in your life beyond what you ever dreamed possible.

Dead Sea Scrolls

Hatshepsut

Ark of The Covenant

Odin

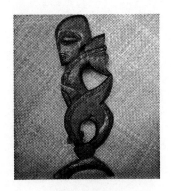

Aumakua

Cherubim

Glossary

Abrahamic Religion – any religion traceable to Abraham, patriarch of the Hebrew Bible primarily including Christianity, Judaism or Islam.

Angel – a celestial being who acts as a messenger of God.

Apocrypha – Greek for 'hidden,' refers to a set of Biblical books approved by the Roman Catholic Church but not listed in the Bible because they were not a part of the original Hebrew Bible.

Applied Kinesiology – see kinesiology

Ark of Covenant – gold plated wooden box from the Hebrew Bible that housed the Ten Commandments.

Aumakua – ancestral gods of the ancient Hawaiian people manifested themselves in the natural world.

Binary divination – system with only two parts such as yes or no.

Book of Changes, *see I-Ching*

Chaos theory –attempts to find order in seemingly disorderly systems and locate the underlying common denominator between them.

Cherubim – second level of nine in the order of angels in the medieval system of angelology. Cherubim adorned the lid of the Ark of the Covenant.

Cherubs –small angels with chubby faces.

Conclave – private meeting of Cardinals to select a new Pope.

Council of Nicea – Three hundred bishops who met in 325 A.D. to determine the outcome of a dispute over Biblical language developed the Nicene Creed which clarified that God and the son, or Christ, were one and the same.

Dead Sea Scrolls- Texts from the Hebrew Bible found between 1947 and 1956 in caves in Qumran near the Dead Sea said to have been authored by the Essenes.

Divining rod – a stick or pole used to locate underground water or mineral deposits.

Doctrine & Covenants – Set of 65 revelations given to Joseph Smith is the foundation for Mormon scriptures.

Dowsing – the ancient art of using a stick to locate underground sources of water or other valuable material resources. In modern times, rods are more commonly used.

Edgar Cayce –considered the world's greatest psychic, Cayce lived in the early to mid 20th century and gave over 14,000 psychic readings while in a deep state of trance.

Exodus – refers to one of the books of Moses in the Bible.

Feng Shui – Ancient Chinese art of special arrangement of objects to be in harmony with the environment.

Futurables –term used in the Catholic Church to describe how God views possibilities that did not occur.

Hatshepsut – Female Egyptian Pharaoh in 18th Dynasty.

Heptoscopy – ancient art of divination through study of the internal organs of animals, especially the liver.

Hexagram –in the I-Ching it is a symbol of six lines composed of two trigrams -three lined figures- designed to give divinatory information.

Holy of Holies - inner chamber of the Tabernacle, or temple, where the priest would go to meet with God.

Huginn - – in Norse mythology, a raven named 'thought' belonging to the god Odin.

I-Ching – ancient Chinese divinatory system may be the oldest book in the world.

Kahuna – name given to any expert in ancient Hawaii, kahunas could be expert in herbs, fishing, canoe building, but in modern times, the term usually refers to the priests.

Kinesiology- study of anatomy and muscle movement.

Lots, casting lots – using an object to make a random determination about something.

Muninn – in Norse mythology, Muninn was a raven named 'memory' belonging to the god Odin.

Muscle Testing – process of accessing the body through the nervous system.

Nag Hammadi – town in Egypt where 13 leather bound codices were found in 1945 containing what is known as the Gnostic Gospels, which include the Gospel of Thomas.

Norse – relating to the area of Scandanavia – Norway, Sweden and Denmark and sometimes Iceland and Finland.

Odin – primary god of Norse Mythology.

Pantheon – word describes the collective set of gods for a particular belief system.

Pearl of Great Price – originally referred to a parable told by Jesus in the Gospel of Matthew later used by Latter Day Saints as the name of one of the primary sets of scripture of the Mormon religion.

Pendulum –any heavy object suspended by a rope or chain used in divination or dowsing.

Pineal gland – endocrine gland in the brain that creates melatonin in the body and linked to psychic awareness.

Rosicrucian –secret organization devoted to ancient philosophical and mystical teachings and their use in modern life.

Runes – once an ancient Germanic alphabet, runes have been used since ancient times for divination purposes.

Septuagint – Greek version of the Hebrew Scriptures from the 3rd Century.

Sub-conscious – the part of the mind that stores our memories outside of conscious awareness.

Super-conscious – refers to the 'higher self' or the part of the self most connected to the Creator or all-knowing self.

Sumerians – people who lived in the area between the Tigris and Euphrates Rivers called Mesopotamia in ancient times, in what is now Modern Turkey.

Synchronicity – Carl Jung's theory about how seemingly random events come together in meaningful ways that defy probability.

Tabernacle – early Christian word for church, temple or place of worship.

Tanakh – the Hebrew scriptures.

Taoism – ancient Chinese philosophy and religion based on teachings of Lao-tzu from the 6th century B.C. recognizing many gods.

Tarot – set of 72 cards used since ancient times for 'entertainment' and fortunetelling.

Thummim – Hebrew for 'perfections.'

Torah – the first five books of the Tanakh, or Hebrew Bible, also the books of Moses.

Trigrams – eight sets of three symbolic lines representing everything in the known universe used in the I-Ching, Chinese Book of Changes, and in Feng Shui.

Urim – Hebrew for 'lights.'

Vulgate – Official Roman Catholic Bible translated from Latin contains books not found in the King James version.

Yang – male aspect of creation – white, sun, positive, aggressive.

Yin – female aspect of creation – black, moon, negative, receptive.

ISIS

Bibliography

Ankerberg, John and John Weldon. *What Do Mormons Really Believe?* Eugene, Oregon: Harvest House Publishers, 2002.

Auden, W.H. *Havamal: Words of the High One.* Princeton, NJ: Princeton University Press, 1930.

Beckwith, Martha. *Hawaiian Mythology.* Honolulu: Hawaii: University of Hawaii Press, 1970.

Berg, Yehuda. *The Power of Kabbalah: Technology for the Soul.* New York: NY: Kabbalah Publishing, 2004.

Berthrong, John H. and Evelyn Nagai. *Confucianism: A Short Introduction.* Oxford, England: Oneworld Publications, 2000.

Besserman, Perle. *The Shambhala Guide to Kabbalah and Jewish Mysticism.* Boston, MA: Shambhala Publications, Inc., 1997.

Betts, Gavin. *Teach Yourself Latin.* London: Hodder Headline Plc, 2000.

Bhaktipada, Swami. *Heart of the Gita.* Moundsville, WV: Palace Publishing, 1990.

Bible: Authorized King James Version, New York, NY: The World Publishing Company, 1945.

Blum, Ralph H. *The Book of Runes.* New York: NY: St. Martin's Press, 1993.

Book of Mormon. Salt Lake City, UT, Church of Jesus Christ of Latter Day Saints.

Braden, Gregg. *The God Code: The Secret of Our Past, the Promise of Our Future*. Carlsbad, CA: Hay House, Inc. 2004.

Braden, Gregg. *The Isaiah Effect: Decoding the Lost Science of Prayer and Prophecy*. New York: NY: Three Rivers Press, 2000.

Brown, Brian. *The Wisdom of the Egyptians*. Sacred-Texts.com, 1923.

Budge, E.A. Wallis. *The Egyptian Book of the Dead*. Sacred-Texts.com, 1895.

Budge, E.A. Wallis. *The Egyptian Heaven and Hell*. Sacred-Texts.com, 1905.

Budge, E.A. Wallis. *An Egyptian Hieroglyphic Dictionary Volume One*. New York, NY: Dover Publications, 1978.

Budge, E.A. Wallis. *The Liturgy of Funerary Offerings*. Sacred-Texts.com, 1909.

Budge, E.A. Wallis. *Legends of the Gods: The Egyptian Texts*. Sacred-Texts.com, 1912.

Bushman, Richard L. *Joseph Smith and the Beginnings of Mormonism*. Chicago, IL: University of Illinois Press, 1984.

Campbell, Joseph. *The Hero with a Thousand Faces*. Princeton, NJ: Princeton University Press, 1949.

Cambell, Joseph. *The Masks of God: Occidental Mythology*. New York, NY: Penguin Books, 1964.

Caradeau, Jean-Luc and Cecile Donner. *The Dictionary of Superstitions*. Paris, France: International Book Promotion, 1984.

Cayce, Edgar. *The Complete Edgar Cayce Readings*. ARE Press, 1999.

Cayce, Edgar Evans, Gail Cayce Schwartzer, and Douglas G Richards. *Mysteries of Atlantis Revisited*. New York, NY: St Martin's Press, 1988.

Charles, R.H. *The Book of Enoch the Prophet*. Boston, MA: Weiser Books, 2003.

Christensen, John. *Smoke Over the Vatican: Picking the Pope: Tellers, Tallies and Antipopes*. CNN.com, 2005.

Cicero, Chic and Sandra Tabitha Cicero. *Self-Initiation into the Golden Dawn Tradition*. St. Paul, MN: Llewellyn Publications, 1998.

Coelho, Paulo. *The Alchemist*. San Francisco, CA: Harper Collins, 1993.

Cooper, J.C. *An Illustrated Encyclopedia of Traditional Symbols*. New York, NY: Thames and Hudson, 1978.

Cotterell, Arthur. *The Encyclopedia of Mythology*. London: Anness Publishing Limited, 1996.

Cotterell, Maurice. *The Tutankhamun Prophecies: The Sacred Secret of the Maya, Egyptians, and Freemasons*. Rochester, Vermont: Bear and Company, 2001.

Craze, Richard. *I-Ching: Book and Card Pack*. New York, NY: Sterling Publishing Company, Inc. 2000.

Crim, Keith, Roger A. Bullard and Larry D. Shinn. *Abingdon Dictionary of Living Religions*. Nashville, TN: Parthenon Press, 1981.

Crury, Nevill. *Shamanism: An Introductory Guide to Living in Harmony with Nature*. Boston, MA: Element Books, 2000.

Crystal, Ellie. *"Egyptian Dream Skrying."* Crystal Links.com, 2005.

Cunningham, Scott. *Cunningham's Encyclopedia of Crystal, Gem & Metal Magic.* St. Paul, MN: Llewellyn Publications, 1988.

Cunningham, Scott. *Earth, Air, Fire & Water.* St. Paul, MN, Llewellyn Publications, 1991.

Cunningham, Scott. *Hawaiian Magic and Spirituality.* St. Paul, MN: Llewellyn Publications, 1994.

Dee, John. *True & Faithful Relation of What Passed for Many Years Between Dr. John Dee and Some Spirits.* London, England: Kessinger Publishing, 1659.

Dennis, James Teackle. *The Burden of Isis*, Sared-Texts.com, 1910.
Duquette, Lon Milo. *The Book or Ordinary Oracles.* Boston, MA: Red Wheel/Weiser Books, 2005.

Doore, Kathy. *The Nazca Spaceport and The Isa Stones of Peru.* Labyrintha.com, 2005.

Easton, M.G. *Easton's Bible Dictionary.* New York, NY: Cosimo, 1897.

Eddy, Mary Baker. *Science and Health with Keys to the Scriptures.* Boston, Massachusetts: First Church of Christ, Scientist, 1917.

Ehananmani (Dr. A.C. Ross). *Mitakuye Oyasin "We are all Related": America Before Columbus Based on the Oral History of 33 Tribes.* Denver, CO: Wiconi Waste, 1989.

Fornander, Abraham. *An Account of the Polynesian Race, Its Origin and Migrations, and the Ancient History of the Hawaiian People to the Time of Kamehameha I.* Honolulu: HI, Bishop Museum, 1878-1885.

Gibran, Kahlil. *The Prophet.* New York, NY: Alfred A. Knopf, 1923.

Guralnik, David B. "*Teraphim*." Webster's New World Dictionary of the American Language: Second College Edition, New York, NY: Simon & Schuster, 1984.

Green, Miranda J. *Dictionary of Celtic Myth & Legend.* New York: NY: Thames & Hudson, 1992.

Griffith, F. LI and Herbert Thompson. *The Demotic Magical Papyrus of London and Leiden.* Sacred-Texts.com, 1904.

Hackin, J. *Asiatic Mythology: A Detailed Description and Explanation of the Mythologies of All the Great Nations of Asia.* New York, NY: Crescent Books, 1932.

Hafen, Leroy and Ann W. Hafen. *Handcarts to Zion: The Story of a Unique Western Migration, 1856-1860.* Lincoln. Nebraska: The University of Nebraska Press, 1992.

Hall, Judy. *Napoleon's Oracle: The Ancient Book of Fate from Egypt's Valley of the Kings.* New York, NY: Barnes & Noble Books, 2003.

Hamilton, Edith. *Mythology.* Boston, MA: Little Brown & Company, 1942.

Hinckley, Gordon B. *Faith: The Essence of True Religion.* Salt Lake City, Utah: The Deseret Book Company, 1989.

Hulse, David Allen. *The Key of It All Book One: The Eastern Mysteries.* St. Paul, MN: Llewellyn Publications, 1993.

Hulse, David Allen. *The Key of It All Book Two: The Western Mysteries.* St. Paul, MN: Llewellyn Publications, 1994.

Kaehr, Shelley. *Edgar Cayce's Guide to Gemstones, Minerals, Metals & More.* Virginia Beach, VA: ARE Press, 2005.

King, Godfre Ray. *Unveiled Mysteries.* Schaumberg, IL: Saint

Germain Press, 1982.

Knight, Gareth. *A Practical Guide to Qabalistic Symbolism*. Boston, MA: Weiser Books, 2001.

Kunz, George Frederick. *The Curious Lore of Precious Stones*. New York, NY: Dover Publications, 1913.

Lewis, Brenda Ralph. *Sutton Pocket Histories: The Aztecs*. Guernsey, Channel Islands: Sutton Publishing, 1999.

Mac Annaidh, Seamas. *Irish History From Prehistoric Times to the Present Day*. Bath, UK: Parragon Publishing, 2002.

Mack, Edward. "*Purim; Pur*," International Standard Bible Encyclopaedia. Edited by James Orr. Blue Letter Bible. 1913. 5 May 2003.

Maharisha Mahesh Yogi. *Bhagavad-Gita: A New Translation and Commentary with Sanskrit Text Chapters 1-6*. London England: Penguin Group, 1967.

Mathers, S.L. MacGregor. *The Book of the Sacred Magic of Abramelin the Mage*. New York, NY: Dover Pubications, Inc., 1900.

Mathers, S.L. MacGregor. *The Key of Solomon the King*. Boston, MA: Weiser Books, 1972.

Mead, Frank S. and Samuel S. Hill. *Handbook of Denominations in the United States*. Nashville, TN: Abingdon Press, 1985.

Mercer, Samuel A.B. *The Pyramid Texts*. Sacred-Texts.com, 1952.

Muller, Klaus E and Ute Ritz-Muller. *Soul of Africa: Magical Rites and Traditions*. Cologne, Germany: Konemann Verlagsgesellschaft MBH, 1999.

Nielsen, Greg. *Beyond Pendulum Power: Entering the Energy World.* Reno, NV: Conscious Books, 1988.

Nielsen, Greg and Joseph Polansky. *Pendulum Power: A Mystery You Can See, a Power You Can Feel.* Rochester, VT: Destiny Books, 1977.

Oldstone-Moore, Jennifer. *Confucianism: Origins, Beliefs, Practices, Holy Texts, Sacred Places.* New York, NY: Oxford University Press, 2002.

Parfitt, Will. *The Elements of The Qabalah.* New York, NY: Barnes & Noble Books, 1991.

Parrinder, Geoffrey. *World Religions From Ancient History to the Present.* New York: NY: Hamlyn Publishing Group Limited, 1971.

Pennick, Nigel. *The Sacred World of the Celts: An Illustrated Guide to Celtic Spirituality and Mythology.* Newton Abbot, Devon: Godsfield Press, 1997.

Pennick, Nigel. *Magical Alphabets: The Secrets and Significance of Ancient Scripts – Including Runes, Greek, Ogham, Hebrew and Alchemical Alphabets.* Boston, MA: Weiser Books, 1992.

Peterson, Joseph H. *John Dee's Five Books of Mystery: Original Sourcebook of Enochian Magic.* Boston, MA: Weiser Books, 2003.

Poignant, Roslyn. *Oceanic Mythology: Polynesia, Micronesia, Melanesia, Australia.* London: Paul Hamlyn, 1967.

Prinz, Martin, George Harlow and Joseph Peters. *Simon & Schuster's Guide to Rocks and Minerals.* New York: NY: Simon & Schuster, 1977.

Regardie, Israel. *777 and Other Qabalistic Writings of Aleister Crowley.* Boston, MA: Weiser Books, 1912.

Regula, DeTraci. *Sacred Scarabs for Divination and Personal Power*. St. Paul, MN: Llewellyn Publications, 2001.

Remler, Pat. *Egyptian Mythology A to Z.* New York, NY: Facts on File, Inc., 2000.

Schumann, Walter. *Gemstones of the World.* New York: NY: Sterling Publishing Co, Inc., 2000.

Seleem, Dr. Ramses. *Egyptian Book of the Dead.* New York, NY: Sterling Publishing, 2001.

Shakir, M.H. *The Qur'an: Translation*. Elmhurst, NY: Tahrike Tarsile Qur'an, Inc., 2003.

Silverman WA, Chalmers I. *Casting and drawing lots: a time-honoured way of dealing with uncertainty and for ensuring fairness.* The James Lind Library (www.jameslindlibrary.org).

Sitchin, Zecharia. *The 12th Planet: Book One of the Earth Chronicles.* New York, NY: Avon Books, 1976.

Smith, Joseph Fielding. *Essentials in Church History: A History of the Church from the Birth of Joseph Smith to the Present Time, with Introductory Chapters on the Antiquity of the Gospel and the "Falling Away."* Salt Lake City: Utah: The Deseret Book Company, 1972.

Spitz, Herman H., and Yves Marcuard. *"Chevreul's Report on the Mysterious Oscillations of the Hand-Held Pendulum."* Skeptical Inquirer, July 2001.

Tanakh: A New Translation of the Holy Scriptures According to Hebrew Text. Jerusalem: The Jewish Publication Society, 1985.

Tauber, Yanki. *"Sixty Days of Purim."* Chabad.org, 2005.

"*Teraphim.*" Free Dictionary.com, 2005.

Too, Lillian. *The Complete Illustrated Guide to Feng Shui: How to Apply the Secrets of Chinese Wisdom for Health, Wealth and Happiness.* Boston, MA: Element Books, 1996.

Twain, Mark. *Christian Science.* Buffalo, NY: Prometheus Books, 1993.

Tyson, Donald. *Enochian Magic for Beginners: The Original System of Angel Magic.* St. Paul, MN: Llewellyn Publications, 1997.

Vermes, Geza. *The Complete Dead Sea Scrolls in English.* New York, NY: Penguin Books, 1962.

Vivian, R. Gwinn and Bruce Hilpert. *The Chaco Handbook: An Encyclopedic Guide.* Salt Lake City, UT: University of Utah Press, 2002.

Walker, Barbara G. *The Woman's Dictionary of Symbols and Sacred Objects.* San Francisco, CA: Harper Collins, 1988.

Wilkinson, Richard H. *The Complete Gods and Goddesses of Ancient Egypt.* New York: NY: Thames & Hudson, 2003.

Wilkinson, Richard H. *The Complete Temples of Ancient Egypt.* New York: NY: Thames & Hudson, 2000.

Yogananda, Paramahansa. *How You Can Talk With God.* Los Angeles, CA: Self Realization Fellowship Publishers, 1957.

Index

Index

About The Author

Dr. Shelley Kaehr is currently one of the world's leading authorities on energy healing and mind-body medicine and the author of six books.

Kaehr recognized the need to educate the public about vibrational medicine and energy healing after surviving a near-death experience several years ago. Shelley noted a severe lack in public awareness about the effects of electromagnetic fields and their effect on health and wellness.

Her work combines energy medicine, past life, and future journeys via hypnosis. Dr. Kaehr believes memories are stored energetically in the subtle fields of the body and that therapeutic interventions must be addressed at both an energetic and verbal level for true healing to occur.

A former sales trainer, public relations specialist, and host of Beyond Reality radio show in Dallas, TX, Kaehr received her Ph.D. in Parapsychic Science from "The American Institute of Holistic Theology" in 2001 and now travels throughout the US and abroad lecturing and conducting thousands of past-life and future memory journeys through hypnosis. Her work has been endorsed by such notables as Dr. Brian Weiss, Gregg Braden, Raymond Moody, M.D., and the Association for Research & Enlightenment.

Order Form

To order your own Urim and Thummim, please complete the form with cashier's check, credit card number or money order and send to:

> An Out of This World Production
> P.O. Box 610943
> Dallas, TX 75261-0943
> Plese print clearly

Name ———————————————————
Address ————————————————
City, State, Zip ——————————————
Phone ———————————————————
e-mail ———————————————————
Mastercard/visa number
expiration date
Credit card billing address (if different from above)

Set comes complete with velvet carrying bag
Only $14 includes shipping and handling!
TX residents, add 8% sales tax.

Or you can order online at
www.galactichealing.org

Printed in the United States
38785LVS00003B/199-510

9 781929 841196